WHEN
THE
HEART
WAITS

WHEN THE HEART WAITS

Spiritual Direction for Life's Sacred Questions

SUE MONK KIDD

HarperSanFrancisco

A Division of HarperCollins*Publishers*

FIRST HARPERCOLLINS PAPERBACK EDITION PUBLISHED IN 1992

Library of Congress Cataloging-in-Publication Data

Kidd, Sue Monk.
   When the heart waits: spiritual direction for life's sacred
  questions / Sue Monk Kidd. — 1st HarperCollins pbk.
     p. cm.
  Originally published: San Francisco: Harper & Row, ©1990.
  ISBN 0–06–064587–3
    1. Spiritual life. 2. Christian life—1960– I. Title.
[BV4501.K427 1992]
248.4—dc20   91–58175
                                          CIP

---

05 RRD(H)

To Sandy,
who has risked newness
along with me

I said to my soul, be still, and wait. . . .
So the darkness shall be the light,
and the stillness the dancing.

T. S. ELIOT

CONTENTS

PREFACE

When the Heart Waits was written from a place deep inside me. It comes out of the well of my own journey and midlife experience. It's always difficult and risky to try to put soulmaking into words. I found that to be especially true with this book. It asked much of me. It called for a painful honesty and vulnerability that I found daunting. It asked me to go deep into myself, to open my story, to invite you into what I can only call a merciful coming together of reader and author.

I've tried to grapple with the sacred questions of life, with the journey and mystery of the human soul as it grows spiritually, moving through passages most have forgotten exist. You'll find me talking a lot about waiting, for in many ways waiting is the missing link in the transformation process. I'm not referring to waiting as we're accustomed to it, but waiting as the passionate and contemplative crucible in which new life and spiritual wholeness can be birthed.

During the past few years, various people have talked with me about spiritual direction for their lives. They've told me that God was summoning them to get in touch with the flow of their interior lives, with the deep and beautiful work of soulmaking. This book is an attempt to help them—and you—with this endeavor.

I've tried to open up a path before you—one grounded in the Bible, in centuries of Christian spiritual writing, and in contemporary spiritual direction and developmental psychology. I've tried to offer down-to-earth truths from my own life, as well as profound truths from the great tradition of Christian spirituality. It has been my task to weave them together to make a tapestry of storytelling and teaching that might open your eyes to the transforming Christ-journey we're all called to make.

My deepest hope is that you'll read not only with your mind but also with your heart, for that is when God strikes music and life into any author's words.

When referring to God, I've used language which highlights that God is neither male or female. Masculine pronouns appear only when I'm quoting from another source.

This book has already been a merciful coming together of many people who helped me during the writing process. First of all, I owe a great debt to my friends and colleagues at Harper & Row, who have been helpful and supportive of my writing. I'm especially grateful to Rebecca Laird, who edited this book and delicately wove for me an environment of creative freedom, direction, and encouragement. A special word of gratitude also goes to Jan Johnson, whose constant support has meant more to me than she knows.

I'm indebted to the many friends who supported me during the writing of this book. To Roy M. Carlisle, who helped me birth the original concept and offered enthusiasm for developing the idea into a book; to the women of Grace Episcopal Church in Anderson, South Carolina, who invited me to address them concerning the themes and material in the book while it was still in progress and whose affirming response gave me new energy toward completing it; to those who "waited" with me through the journey I describe in the book—John, Betty, and Mary Page. They supplied listening hearts and a loving participation in my story.

I thank Betty Blackerby, who has become the sister I never had. Her presence and the sharing of her own experience have graced me and this project.

I'm grateful to my children, Bob and Ann, for their patience as I wrote, as well as for the richness of their lives, which overflows into these pages. My deepest thank-you goes to my husband,

Sandy, for believing in me and in this book throughout. His love, help, and encouragement have been an immense gift.

Today is the Feast Day of St. Francis of Assisi. As I finish this book, I think of one particular line from his beautiful prayer: "Where there is darkness, let me sow light." May it be so.

Sue Monk Kidd
Anderson, South Carolina

WHEN
THE
HEART
WAITS

WAITING AND TRANSFORMATION

CHAPTER 1

The Long Way Round

Midway this way of life we're bound upon,
I woke to find myself in a dark wood,
Where the right road was wholly lost and gone. . . .
It is so bitter it goes nigh to death.

DANTE

Patience is everything.

RAINER MARIA RILKE

Overhead a thickening of clouds wreathed everything in grayness. It was February, when the earth of South Carolina seems mired in the dregs of winter. I had been walking for miles; I don't know how many. I could feel neither my toes inside my shoes nor the wind on my face. I could feel nothing at all but an intense aching in my soul.

For some months I had been lost in a baffling crisis of spirit. Back in the autumn I had awakened to a growing darkness and cacophony, as if something in my depths were crying out. A whole chorus of voices. Orphaned voices. They seemed to speak for all the unlived parts of me, and they came with a force and dazzle that I couldn't contain. They seemed to explode the boundaries of my existence. I know now that they were the clamor of a new self struggling to be born.

MIDLIFE DARKNESS

I was standing on the shifting ground of midlife, having come upon that time in life when one is summoned to an inner transformation, to a crossing over from one identity to another. When change-winds swirl through our lives, especially at midlife, they often call us to undertake a new passage of the spiritual journey: that of confronting the lost and counterfeit places within us and releasing our deeper, innermost self—our *true* self. They call us to come home to ourselves, to become who we really are.

That winter of my discontent, I had no real idea of any of this. I was mystified by the inner upheaval I felt. This sort of thing *couldn't* be happening to me, I told myself. I had already been on an inner spiritual quest—one that had begun eight years earlier with an experience of chest pains and stress. My journey had taught me a more contemplative way of being in the world and had given me the first real centeredness I'd known. Discovering myself loved by God and forging new dimensions of intimacy with God's presence had brought much healing to my fragmented life.

I should have remembered, though, that the life of the spirit is never static. We're born on one level, only to find some new struggle toward wholeness gestating within. That's the sacred intent of life, of God—to move us continuously toward growth, toward recovering all that is lost and orphaned within us and restoring the divine image imprinted on our soul. And rarely do significant shifts come without a sense of our being lost in dark woods, or in what T. S. Eliot called the "vacant interstellar spaces."[1]

I kept walking through the fogged afternoon light as if the mere ritual of putting one foot in front of the other would lead me out of my pain. I buried my hands in the pockets of my coat and watched the wind blow a paper cup along the gutter. I was approaching the college campus. Was it possible that I had walked so far? The sun was beginning to fade now. I started to turn back but felt weighted inside, as if I couldn't move.

I dragged myself to a little bench wedged among the trees. Sitting there, I studied their bony arms and felt their emptiness, their desperate reach for sky and light. Tears rimmed my eyes and burned on my cheeks. It made no sense. I'd never really believed in midlife crises. They had seemed too trendy, another cliché-ridden piece of Americana. But here I was having one, and it was frighteningly real.

The familiar circles of my life left me with a suffocating feeling. My marriage suddenly seemed stale, unfulfilling; my religious structures, stifling. Things that used to matter no longer did; things that had never mattered were paramount. My life had curled up into the frightening mark of a question.

Each day I went about my responsibilities as always, writing through the morning and early afternoon, picking my children up from school, answering mail, shopping for groceries, cooking— plowing through the never-ending list of duties. I've always been accomplished at being dutiful (even during a crisis). Outwardly I appeared just fine. Inside I was in turmoil.

My husband, Sandy, was as exasperated by my experience as he was bewildered. He wanted things to go back to the comfortable way they were before. He wanted me to "snap out of it." I did too, of course. I had ordered myself to do just that numerous times. But it was sort of like looking at an encroaching wave and telling it to recede. Demanding didn't make it happen.

I sighed, my mind wandering to the picture I'd sketched the night before. (I have a hobby of charcoal drawing, and lately I'd found solace in my sketch pad.) The previous evening I'd drawn a tent in the middle of some wind-howling woods. The stakes that secured the bottom of the tent were uprooted, and the flaps were flailing in the wind. As I put down my pencil, I said to myself, "That's my life." Indeed, it seemed as if the stakes that had secured my neat, safe existence—stakes that I had spent most of my life carefully nailing down—had been pulled up, and everything was tossing about. Underneath the sketch I wrote, "Midlife."

Now, as I thought of the drawing, I recognized what a tent dweller I had been. Maybe I was supposed to go wandering in a new part of my inner landscape. Maybe *that's* what midlife was about: pilgrimage.

I drew up the collar of my coat and thought of my external, everyday self—the self I presented to the world. I contemplated the masks I'd worn, the "inner selves" or dominant patterns embedded within me that had influenced my way in the world.

Referring to this multiplicity of inner selves that inhabit each person, Elizabeth O'Conner wrote, "It was during a time of painful conflict that I first began to experience myself as more than one. It was as though I sat in the midst of many selves."[2]

I too sat in the midst of many selves. The Pleaser, the Performer, the Perfectionist—my trinity of P's. I was learning how closely these old roles were connected to another powerful role that I played out: the Good Little Girl.

She was that part of me that had little self-validation or autonomy, who tended to define life by others and their expectations, by collective values and projections. As a woman I sometimes felt that I had been scripted to be all things to all people. But when I tried, I usually ended up forfeiting my deepest identity, my own unique truth as God's creature.

My Good Little Girl endured everything sweetly, feared coloring outside of the traditional lines, and frequently cut herself off from her real thoughts and feelings. She was well adapted to thinking other people's thoughts and following the path of least resistance.

At times she seemed like an orchid in a hothouse: fragile, pleasing, someone who always ended up being pressed between the pages of *someone else's* scrapbook. Much of my life I'd found my principal roles expressed mainly in the pages of someone else's life. I was someone's mother, someone's wife, someone's Sunday school teacher, someone's employee. Wonderful things. But down deep, at soul level, who was *I*?

Now, oddly, I could feel the intimations of an unknown woman locked away inside of me who wanted life and breath, who wanted to shed what wasn't real and vital and recover that which was. I felt the vibrations of a deeper, authentic self who wanted to live out her own unique vision of individuality and embrace her own mystery. Who was this self inside of me who cried out to be?

During the previous few weeks I had been reading the poetry of T. S. Eliot, who at times seemed like a soulmate to me. In his "Love Song of J. Alfred Prufrock" I found my story, the quiet agony of someone who came upon an unsuspecting darkness buried in midlife and met the overwhelming question: "Do I dare/Disturb the universe?/...I have measured out my life with coffee spoons;/ I know the voices dying with a dying fall/Beneath the music from a farther room."[3]

My life felt measured out in lumps too small. And there was a bewitching music from a distant room I couldn't find. Voices dying to be heard. Did I dare disturb the universe within myself?

Believe me, I wanted to shove all this away and pretend it didn't exist. But I couldn't. Life tasted of cardboard and smelled of stagnant air. At times I found myself shut in a closet of pain, unable to find the door. In my blackest moments I actually fantasized about running away from home to find the vital part of me that I had lost.

ENTERING THE QUESTION

As I sat on the bench that day beneath the low-slung gray sky, everything was fomenting, turning end over end like the paper cup I had watched in the street. And suddenly, at the height of my chaos, I began to entertain the overwhelming question confronting me. I had been circling it for a long while, but now, at last, I walked right into the center of it. It was a dangerous thing to do, for those who enter the heart of a sacred question and feel the searing heat it gives off are usually compelled to live on into the answer.

Is it possible, I asked myself, *that I'm being summoned from some deep and holy place within? Am I being asked to enter a new passage in the spiritual life—the journey from false self to true self? Am I being asked to dismantle old masks and patterns and unfold a deeper, more authentic self—the one God created me to be? Am I being compelled to disturb my inner universe in quest of the undiscovered being who clamors from within?*

Unfortunately, there has been little emphasis on this summons within Christian circles. When it comes, we don't understand that we're being thrust into personal transformation, into the task of birthing an "I" that is not yet. We write it off as just another predicament or plight—perhaps the result of burnout or our dissatisfaction with life.

I believe, however, that in such a summons we're actually being presented with a spiritual developmental task. We're being asked to unfold a deeper self—what we might call the life of Christ within us.

To embark on this task involves a deep and profound movement of soul that takes us from an identification with the collective "they" to a discovery of the individual "I," and finally, as we shall eventually see, to an embracing of the compassionate "we." This task is truly one of the more precarious and mysterious pathways in the spiritual life, for how it's navigated radically affects one's alignment with oneself, with God, and with the world.

As I reflected on my struggle that afternoon, my thoughts turned to the discoveries I'd made in the writings of Swiss psychiatrist C. G. Jung. I had been studying his works in earnest for the previous four years. A friend had suggested that I was looking for truth in unorthodox places, but that, of course, is where God often puts it.

Back at the beginning of my spiritual journey I had read avidly through the Western spiritual classics, finding heroes in St. Teresa of Avila, John of the Cross, Julian of Norwich, Meister Eckhart, and especially the contemporary monk and writer Thomas Merton. Again and again I had read about the contemplative journey into God that entails entering the depths of oneself. Later, when I began to read Jung, I was staggered at how much of his work in depth psychology paralleled the spirituality I'd come to know, and at how they enriched one another.

Jung believed that "every midlife crisis is a spiritual crisis, that we are called to die to the old self (ego), the fruit of the first half of life and liberate the new man or woman within us."[4] Here is a hidden and misunderstood turning point of the soul, I thought. Sadly, not every person will maneuver its convoluted mazes. Would I?

I recalled Jung's words in "Stages of Life":

Wholly unprepared, they embark upon the second half of life. Or are there perhaps colleges for forty-year-olds which prepare them for their coming life and its demands as the ordinary colleges introduce our young people to a knowledge of the world and of life? No, there are none. Thoroughly unprepared we take the step into the afternoon of life; worse still, we take this step with the false presupposition that our truths and ideas will serve as hitherto. But we cannot live the afternoon of life according to the programme of life's morning—for what was great in the morning will be little at evening, and what in the morning was true will at evening have become a lie.[5]

Jung divided life into two phases. The first phase, or "morning," is reserved for relating and orienting to the outer world by developing the ego. The second half, or "afternoon," is for adapting to the inner world by developing the full and true self. The midlife transition between these two Jung likened to a difficult birth.

This transition is difficult because it involves a real breakdown of our old spiritual and psychic structures—the old masks and personas that have served us well in the past but that no longer fit. The overarching roles that created the theme song for my life—Perfectionist, Performer, Pleaser, Good Little Girl, submissive churchgoer, passive and traditional wife—began to lose their music. It's anguish to come to that place in life where you know all the words but none of the music.

In our youth we set up inner myths and stories to live by, but around the midlife juncture these patterns begin to crumble. It feels to us like a collapsing of all that is, but it's a holy quaking. "When order crumbles," writes John Shea, "Mystery rises."[6]

One of my favorite pieces of Scripture comes from Ecclesiastes. "To everything there is a season, and a time to every purpose under the heaven: a time to be born, and a time to die; *a time to plant, and a time to pluck up that which is planted*" (Eccles. 3:1–2, KJV, emphasis added). We need reassurance that it's okay to let the old masks die, to "pluck up" what was planted long ago.

I often need permission to do daring things. And when I can't get it from myself, God often sends someone else to give it to me. As I struggled with whether to embrace this experience or banish it, a friend said to me, "If you think God leads you only beside still waters, think again. God will also lead you beside turbulent waters. If you have the courage to enter, you'll think you're drowning. But actually you're being churned into something new. It's okay, Sue, dive in."

When the fullness of time comes, a sacred voice at the heart of us cries out, shaking the old foundation. It draws us into a turbulence that forces us to confront our deepest issues. It's as if some inner, divine grace seeks our growth and becoming and will plunge us, if need be, into a cauldron that seethes with questions and voices we would just as soon not hear. One way or another, the false roles, identities, and illusions spill over the sides of our life, and we're forced to stand in the chaos.

Without such upheaval we would likely go on as always. It's so like us to deny things until some jolting moment—something we call an "eye-opening" experience—comes along and sharpens our vision.

"There is a self within each one of us aching to be born," says theologian Alan Jones.[7] And when this aching breaks into our lives—whether through a midlife struggle or some other crisis—we must somehow find the courage to say yes. Yes to this more real, more Christ-like self struggling to be born.

I leaned back on the little bench that cold February day and tried very hard to say yes to what was struggling inside me. A tree limb made shadows on the sidewalk at my feet. I watched them, remembering for some reason that my daughter, Ann, and I had recently bought the classic *Peter Pan* by J. M. Barrie and were reading it together. I began to think of Peter, the eternal little boy who had a habit of secretly visiting a nursery window along a quiet street to listen to Wendy tell bedtime stories to the children. On one of his trips the dog, Nana, nipped off his shadow as he escaped. One night Peter came back, searching for his shadow. He found it at last, buried away in a box, and with the help of Wendy sewed it back on.

It seemed to me that my quest was to find the part of me I had lost while leaning on a nursery window along a quiet street. The shadow represented an essential part of me buried in darkness— the part hidden beneath the masks and fabrications. Jung said that we all have a "shadow"; it's the rejected, inferior person inside we've always ignored and fought becoming.[8]

I kept wishing for a "Wendy"—some wise, loving helper—to come and gently stitch it back. In fact, I'd sought a counselor for help. We talked of the crossing over at midlife, the spiritual revisioning that's called for. But I hadn't yet been able to find my own vision of transformation, or even believe that it was possible. How would it happen? What was I being asked to do?

CALL TO WAITING

I sat there in the brooding cold and knew that my family would be wondering what had happened to me. I had left them back at home beside a fire smoldering on the grate. "When will you be back?" Sandy had asked when I left. "What about dinner?"

Dinner? *Dinner?* "Who cares about dinner?" I'd wanted to cry. But I didn't. I simply said, "Can't you please start it? I really *have* to take a walk."

But what had my walk accomplished? I tried to pray. "Please, God...please." I muttered the words, trusting that God would distill the meaning from them and break through my terrible impasse. A gust rippled through the tree limbs and sang a song of absence. It was too much for me. I got up and walked away.

I burrowed into the wind, my head down. I happened to look up again as I passed beneath the branches of a dogwood tree, and my eyes fell upon a curious little appendage suspended from a twig just over my head.

I kept walking. *No, stop...look closer.* Not knowing what else to do but obey the inner impulse, I backed up and looked again. I took one step toward it, then two, until I was so close that the fog of my breath encircled it. *I had come upon a cocoon.*

I was caught suddenly by a sweep of reverence, by a sensation that made me want to sink to my knees. For somehow I knew that I had stumbled upon an epiphany, a strange gracing of my darkness. I took my forefinger and touched the botton tip of the tiny brown chrysalis and felt something like light move in me. In that moment God seemed to speak to me about transformation. About the descent and emergence of the soul. About hope.

I broke the twig from the limb and carried the chrysalis home. For this was *my* cocoon. My darkness. My soul incubating within.

Back home I carefully taped the twig with the cocoon to the branch of a crab-apple tree in my backyard. Then I went inside.

The children were engrossed in their homework, and Sandy was setting the table. I stood at the window watching the cocoon, which hung in the winter air like an upside-down question mark. *Live* the question, God whispered.

That was the moment the knowledge descended into my heart and I understood. *Really* understood. Crisis, change, all the myriad upheavals that blister the spirit and leave us groping—they aren't voices simply of pain but also of creativity. And if we would only listen, we might hear such times beckoning us to a season of waiting, to the place of fertile emptiness.

I turned from the window, quickened by the moment. I knew. Dear God, I knew. I must enter the chrysalis.

THE SPIRITUAL ART OF COCOONING

The Greek word for *soul* is *psyche*, and is often symbolized as a *butterfly*. Both the soul and the butterfly are metamorphosed. While it was tempting for me to think that the growth and emergence of my authentic self would happen with little time or effort on my part, that isn't so. The fullness of one's soul evolves slowly. We're asked to go within to gestate the newness God is trying to form; we're asked to collaborate with grace.

That doesn't mean that grace isn't a gift. Nor does it mean that the deliberate process of waiting *produces* grace. But waiting *does* provide the time and space necessary for grace to happen. Spirit needs a container to pour itself into. Grace needs an arena in which to incarnate. Waiting can be such a place, if we allow it.

Not long ago I came upon a poster hanging in an art shop. On it was a golden butterfly, its wings spread against a blaze of sky. "Your soul is your greatest work of art," the caption read. As I looked more closely, however, I noticed in the bottom lefthand corner of the poster the husk of an empty cocoon, a painful reminder that bright wings and works of art don't just happen. They require the courage to let go and spin the chrysalis. In soulmaking we can't bypass the cocoon. Wherever there are bright new wings, there's always the husk of waiting somewhere in the corner.

During the days after my February walk, I asked myself what would happen if I could learn the spiritual art of cocooning. Might I discover a stilling of the soul that invites God and a new re-creation of life? Would I see that waiting, with all its quiet passion and hidden fire, is the real crucible of spiritual transformation? Would the posture of the cocoon allow me a way to shed old, embedded patterns of living and move into a more genuine humanity where the authentic self breaks through?

I wondered if waiting was the "missing link" in spiritual evolving, the lost and forgotten experience crucial to becoming fully human, fully Christian, fully ourselves.

One day, while I was reading in the Gospels, it occurred to me that when important times of transition came for Jesus, he entered enclosures of waiting—the wilderness, a garden, the tomb. Jesus' life was a balanced rhythm of waiting on God and expressing the fruits of that waiting.

I had tended to view waiting as mere passivity. When I looked it up in my dictionary however, I found that the words *passive* and *passion* come from the same Latin root, *pati*, which means "to endure." Waiting is thus both passive and passionate. It's a vibrant, contemplative work. It means descending into self, into God, into the deeper labyrinths of prayer. It involves listening to disinherited voices within, facing the wounded holes in the soul, the denied and undiscovered, the places one lives falsely. It means struggling with the vision of who we really are in God and molding the courage to live that vision.

Coming upon the cocoon initiated me into an intensity I couldn't have imagined. That I stumbled upon it at all seems to me a tender miracle, a synchronicity that points to the sheer eloquence of life's ability to speak to us.

For over a year I lived and worked inwardly with the symbology of caterpillar, chrysalis, and butterfly. I accepted them as God's gift to me—healing symbols that went beyond the usual sentimentality attached to them. We tend to forget, I think, the power of a symbol to mediate grace and move us toward change.

From the moment that I embraced these images they appeared and reappeared outwardly. Suddenly they were everywhere I looked. They came to me unbidden as gifts—on cards, wrapping paper, necklaces, books, paperweights, posters, key chains, glass figures, drawings. Wandering about New York, I "happened upon" a butterfly gallery that had nothing in it but artistic panels of mounted butterflies. I brought two of them home to adorn my desk. The symbols also came to me repeatedly in my dreams. And not once, or even twice, but three times a real butterfly paused to light upon me. Such were life's inexplicable but eloquent anointings. Frankly, the whole thing became a holy hilarity. "All right, all *right*, God," I wanted to shout, "I get it!"

STAYING IN THE CIRCLE

The night after my discovery of the cocoon I had a memorable dream. In the Bible, dreams are one of the most significant ways through which God communicates. Episcopal priest and psychologist Morton Kelsey has pointed out that the Christian church has tended to forget the religious value of dreams.[9] For some time I had been coming to appreciate and understand how dreams arising from the unconscious contained revelations and symbolic images opening us to a deeper spiritual realm. Indeed, the dream I had that night held extraordinary meaning.

This is how I recorded it the next morning:

I'm sitting alone reading the newspaper. I turn to the classified ads, hoping that I'll discover something new for my life. Suddenly I come upon an article that announces my death. I'm stunned. How did my obituary get in the want-ads, I wonder?

Through the window I see a white-haired old woman approaching my door. She's carrying yards and yards of lavendar cloth. When she knocks, I open the door. She smiles at me from a wise, weathered face, and I invite her in.

Quietly she begins to twine the purple cloth around me as if I were a mummy. I try to wriggle free. "Still yourself," she tells me sternly. "It is time."

I grow still and silent. She wraps me from head to foot. Then she draws a circle on the floor and places me inside it. "Stand here until I come back," she instructs.

My face is covered, but I see her dimly as she leaves. When she turns, I notice that she has a lavender butterfly sewn on her back.

I woke up abruptly, my heart pounding. The chrysalis in the tree had become the chrysalis within.

The imagery of that dream dancing up from my own depths— and choreographed, I think, by God—laid bare my path, a path universal to everyone who encounters shifting ground and searches the "classifieds," hoping for something new for their lives.

We discover that the only way to achieve newness is to read our own obituary—to die to the old and open the door to the knock of waiting, to allow ourselves to be sheathed in the experience of incubating what needs be born. We find that we must trust the process enough to go into the circle and stay there until the time comes for emergence.

Each morning of that winter, and even sometimes in the cold twilight, I walked outside to the crab-apple tree and gazed at the cocoon. Somehow it helped me find the courage to do what God seemed to be asking. To stay in the circle without escaping, to "still myself" and wait.

One day Ann went with me to see the cocoon. "Remember Stripe and Yellow?" she asked.

I nodded, a smile crossing my face. Stripe and Yellow were two caterpillars in Trina Paulus's book *Hope for the Flowers*. It was the story of how they became butterflies.

Yellow had seen another caterpillar spinning a cocoon and asked, "If I decide to become a butterfly...what do I do?"

"Watch me," came the reply. "I'm making a cocoon. It looks like I'm hiding, I know, but a cocoon is no escape. It's an in-between house where the change takes place....During the change, it will seem...that nothing is happening, but the butterfly is already becoming. It just takes time."[10]

Yellow had been afraid, but she took the risk and spun her own cocoon, later to emerge and unfold her wings.

As I remembered the story, Ann pointed to the cocoon. "Mama, do you think there's a Stripe or a Yellow inside there?"

Suddenly tears rimmed my eyes. "Oh, I hope so," I told her. "I *hope* so."

From then on, the simple yet profound words of that story followed me: "A cocoon is no escape....It just takes time."

A young monk once asked Abba Moses, one of the desert fathers, how to find true spiritual growth. "Go sit in your cell," said the monk, "and it will teach you everything."[11] Somehow we've lost this important secret in the spiritual life—that in "stayed-ness," as George Fox called it, we find the realm for transformation. In the stayed-ness of waiting we find everything we need in order to grow. Suspended upside down in the heart of the question, we touch the sacred spaces of real becoming.

The dangers of leaving a cocoon too soon are obvious. My counselor told me a story about a child who found a cocoon. Wishing to set the creature inside free, he took his pocket knife and pared an opening at the bottom of the chrysalis, making it possible for the butterfly to wriggle free. But when the creature unfurled its wings, it couldn't fly. With the butterfly's waiting cut short, its wings were hopelessly unformed.

The call not only to wait, but to "stay" in my waiting, had arrived. Gradually I would discover what this dark and mysterious process was all about.

THE LONG WAY ROUND

When I was a child, a woman named Sweet worked for our family. She cared for my brothers and me as if we were her own. One day, when we were playing at my grandmother's house, we discovered a wheelbarrow full of rain water. Swimming through it were hundreds of tadpoles.

We raced inside and asked Sweet for three jars. As she was handing them out, my grandmother appeared in the door. "Girls don't catch tadpoles," she said with a laugh. "Sue, you come along with me and I'll teach you to play 'Chopsticks' on the piano." My brothers dashed off to the wheelbarrow, and I ended up at the piano bench.

A few days later Sweet and I started out on one of our frequent walks to the city park about four blocks from my house. The park was the best of places, and I was anxious to get there. But that day Sweet took my hand and started in the wrong direction. "We're taking the long way round," she told me.

The *long* way? The words fell like a curse on my ears. Why would we deliberately go the long way? I made a small scene, but Sweet didn't relent. Off we went the long way. Not four blocks, but eight!

We had walked at least six, when she stopped beside a ditch swollen with water and tadpoles. She pulled a Mason jar from her pocket, one with nail holes in the lid. "Now aren't you glad we took the long way round? Ain't no tadpoles the short way," she said.

Inside my head I heard my grandmother's words: "Only boys catch tadpoles." Only boys. I hesitated, but Sweet nudged me with the jar. Soon I was elbow-deep in the brown water, chasing after the rich, darting life before me. I was reveling in a new universe, and it was one of the grander times of my girlhood. It was the day I learned to challenge the tight, tidy categories of what was expected and possible in my world. Like the tadpoles, I was molting into a new being.

But when I grew up and left home, I began once more to be hammered into tight, tidy spaces of traditional expectation. I learned to conform to roles and wear all sorts of masks that hid my real self. I forgot all about the tadpole experience.

One day early in my cocooning I read a poem by Henry David Thoreau, America's solitary walker, entitled "Among the Worst of Men That Ever Lived." The last line of it struck like the bow of a ship hitting a tiny island submerged in my memory. The line read, "We went on to heaven the long way round."[12]

Dear God, I thought, *the long way round*. The words brought back that long-lost walk to the park, the tadpoles, and Sweet's lyrical voice singing to me, "Now aren't you glad we took the long way round? Ain't no tadpoles the short way." The lesson was fresh upon me again: be your true, unfettered, God-given self, regardless of the expectations hammered into you.

It seemed to me that Sweet and Thoreau had touched upon the same genius. Transformations come only as we go the long way round, only as we're willing to walk a different, longer, more arduous, more inward, more prayerful route. When you wait, you're deliberately choosing to take the long way, to go eight blocks instead of four, trusting that there's a transforming discovery lying pooled along the way.

"Nothing can be more useful to a man than a determination not to be hurried," Thoreau wrote at age twenty-five.[13] He decided to turn away from the "lives of quiet desperation" he saw all around him and march to his own "different drummer," to go to heaven the long way round. On February 8, 1857, Thoreau wrote this in his journal: "You think I am impoverishing myself by withdrawing from men, but in my solitude I have woven for myself a silken web or chrysalis, and nymph-like, shall ere long burst forth a more perfect creature."[14]

In his commentary on Thoreau's work, Robert Bly says that "agreeing to a waiting period is part of it."[15] It's part of the process of leaving the petty life, the false life, the old life.

God is offering an invitation. A call to waiting. A call to the mysteries of the cocoon. I discovered that in the spiritual life, the long way round is the saving way. It isn't the quick and easy religion we're accustomed to. It's deep and difficult—a way that leads into the vortex of the soul where we touch God's transformative powers. But we have to be patient. We have to let go and tap our creative stillness. Most of all, we have to trust that our scarred hearts really do have wings.

CHAPTER 2

Quickaholic Spirituality

Waiting patiently in expectation is the foundation of the spiritual life.
SIMONE WEIL

There is nothing instant or automatic in spiritual development.
ALAN JONES

Winter lumbered toward spring. Outside in my yard, the little cocoon hung in silence. Wait, God seemed to whisper. But another voice rose up in me and around me, a sensible, collective voice insisting that waiting was a huge procrastination, an anachronism, a nice idea, maybe, but something misplaced in the fast-paced, demanding world of today.

Besides, I didn't *want* to wait. Waiting seemed the rawest kind of agony. I wanted God to simply whisk away the masks I had spent most of my life fashioning, to hoist up from my repressed well the lost and neglected parts of myself, to solve my problems, heal my wounds, and alleviate the inexplicable sense of discontent and pain I was feeling. And mind you, I wanted all of this *now*, immediately, or at the very least soon.

I was a typical quickaholic. We are, I suspect, one of the fastest-growing populations around.

It was at this point that I traveled to St. Meinrad Archabbey for a retreat. One day after morning prayers, I walked to the edge of the pond and sat on the grass. I listened to the wind sigh over the water and tried to be still, to simply be there and wait in the moment. But almost instantly my inner chaos rose up. The need to keep moving, to act, to solve everything overpowered me. I got to my feet.

As I returned to the guest quarters, I noticed a monk, ski cap pulled over his ears, sitting perfectly still beneath a tree. There was such reverence in his silhouette, such tranquil sturdiness, that I paused to watch. He was the picture of waiting.

Later I sought him out. "I saw you today sitting beneath the tree—just sitting there so still. How is it that you can wait so patiently in the moment? I can't seem to get used to the idea of doing nothing."

He broke into a wonderful grin. "Well, there's the problem right there, young lady. You've bought into the cultural myth that when you're waiting you're doing nothing."

Then he took his hands and placed them on my shoulders, peered straight into my eyes and said, "I hope you'll hear what I'm about to tell you. I hope you'll hear it all the way down to your toes. When you're waiting, you're *not* doing nothing. You're doing the most important something there is. You're allowing your soul to grow up. If you can't be still and wait, you can't become what God created you to be."

Somehow I knew in my soul that his words were God's words.

That's when I began to probe and question the "cultural myths" that colored my experience of waiting. What were those myths, and how had I bought into them?

THE INSTANT SOCIETY

We live in an age of acceleration, in an era so seduced by the instantaneous that we're in grave danger of losing our ability to wait. Life moves at a staggering pace. Computers yield up immediate answers. Pictures develop before our eyes. Satellites beam television signals from practically anywhere, allowing far-away images to appear instantly in our living rooms. Complex life issues are routinely introduced, dealt with, and solved in neat thirty-minute segments on television.

Space travel, fax machines, instant coffee, disposable diapers. In ways large and small, we're all encapsulated in a speeding world. We're surrounded by express lanes, express mail, express credit. There aren't just restaurants, but "fast-food" restaurants; not simply markets, but "jiffy" markets. Faster is better. Ask most anyone.

The modern person tends to live by appointment calendars. I'm embarrassed at how huge my calendar used to be. I had two pages for every day so that I could "design" time the way I wanted—segment it, save it, manage it, stretch it. Since we have designer clothes and designer chocolate, I suppose it's inevitable that we would want designer time too.

We keep dreaming up ways to conserve time and make it hassle-free. I recently saw an exercise bike with a computer attached so that people can get fit while they work; and last week, while thumbing through a catalogue, I noticed a video entitled "Discover Yourself in Less Than Thirty Minutes."

A study conducted in Pittsburgh timed clerks in major fast-food restaurants to determine which chain served a hamburger, fries, and a soft drink the quickest. The winner took forty-six seconds; the loser, a slow three minutes. Apparently such information is important to a society that places its highest premium on the quick and easy.

Quick and *easy* are magical words with enormous seductive powers. Advertisers know that if they put them on a product it sells better—whether the product is instant potatoes, instant money, or instant relief. We're told that we can walk off ten pounds in two weeks, melt off five inches in five days, or just take a pill and do it overnight. We've been lured by promises of getting new glasses in an hour, an oil change in thirty minutes, and a pizza in twenty.

Is it any wonder that we're fine-tuned from an early age to seek out the instant fix? We want life to respond like our microwave ovens.

Last week my daughter plopped down on the den floor in front of the television to do her homework. She held the remote control in one hand and her math book in the other. "I hate math," she said. "It's so hard." Then, in a moment of mischievous whimsy, she aimed the remote at her homework and pressed the fast-forward button. "Wouldn't it be great to just speed up the hard stuff?" she said. Ah, yes. I know that little fantasy well.

SHORTCUT RELIGION

It was inevitable that the lure of the quick and easy would seep into religion. Our churches have filled up with people looking for sudden and painless paths to change and growth—for what Dietrich Bonhoeffer called "cheap grace."

A lot of us have spent our lives in shortcut religion. We haven't been willing to face the fact that while the spiritual journey is joyous and full, it's also long and hard. It asks much—*too* much sometimes.

Anthony Bloom reminds us that the aim of prayer is nothing less than a "deep change in the whole of our personality." As Thomas Merton says, our commitment is to become "a completely new person." Such extraordinary movements of re-creation don't happen spontaneously or without effort and pain.

When my son was fourteen he experienced an episode of leg pains that kept him awake at night. The doctor pronouned them as "growing pains." I didn't know that such things actually existed. But I sat by Bob's bed in the darkest part of the night and rubbed his shins while he moaned and ached. One night he looked at me and said, "It hurts to grow."

I smiled, unaware then that he was offering me a profound life truth. "But you always said you wanted to be six feet tall," I reminded him.

"Yeah," he muttered, "but I'd like to do it without all this."

He wanted what we all want: a shortcut, someway to bypass the misery and *still* be six feet tall. To grow up spiritually means having growing pains in the darkest part of the night.

Some Christians (even some churches) have responded to this difficult truth by trying to create shortcuts—promises of easy grace, push-button answers to complicated problems, illusions that we can go to church and work to bring in the kingdom out there in the world without entering the fiery process of bringing it into our own soul.

A woman who used to work at a fast-food restaurant once commented that the people who lined up at her register sometimes reminded her of people lining up in church on Sunday morning. They seemed to be looking for the same thing—a quick and easy way to reduce the hunger inside. "Mac-faith," she called it.

Worst of all, that need for a quick fix glared at me from my own life. Wasn't I craving formulaic answers and swift solutions to deep problems? I yearned for an express spirituality that would work at the same speed as my computer, providing a ready transformation and answers to my prayers. Frankly, I resented the fact that God didn't work that way when everything else in my world did.

What has happened to our ability to dwell in unknowing, to live inside a question and coexist with the tensions of uncertainty? Where is our willingness to incubate pain and let it birth something new? What has happened to patient unfolding, to endurance? These things are what form the ground of waiting. And if you look carefully, you'll see that they're also the seedbed of creativity and growth—what allows us to do the daring and to break through to newness. As Thomas Merton observed, "The imagination should be allowed a certain amount of time to browse around."[1]

Creativity flourishes not in certainty but in questions. Growth germinates not in tent dwelling but in upheaval. Yet the seduction is always security rather than venturing, instant knowing rather than deliberate waiting.

I once visited a church where the preacher invited people with heartaches and problems to come to the altar. "God will take care of what's bothering you right now," he proclaimed. Not a word about the desert that lies between our wounds and our healing, our questions and our answers, our departure and our arrival. Nothing about the slow, sacred rhythms of spiritual becoming or the spiral of descent and ascent that make up waiting.

When it comes to religion today, we tend to be long on butterflies and short on cocoons. Somehow we're going to have to relearn that the deep things of God don't come suddenly. It's as if we imagine that all of our spiritual growth potential is dehydrated contents to which we need only add some holy water to make it instantly and easily appear.

I received a letter recently from someone who was feeling impatient about taking the long way round. She wrote, "Pole vaulting is so much more alluring than crawling."

We live in a spiritual environment that tends to emphasize full-blown newness and a sense of "arrival" in the mere time it takes to walk the length of a church aisle. Walking an aisle can be a marvelous thing, as long as we acknowledge that the aisle doesn't end at the altar but goes on winding through life. We seem to have focused so much on exuberant beginnings and victorious endings that we've forgotten about the slow, sometimes tortuous, unraveling of God's grace that takes place in the "middle places."

Professor at Duke Divinity, John H. Westerhoff, discusses this process of unraveling:

> No aspect of thinking on conversion is more foreign to the American evangelical experience than this stress on conversion as a process.... Evangelicals emphasize emotion and an initial movement. This moment is celebrated, recalled, and when the experience fades, recaptured. But Christian tradition does not agree.... Conversion is a continuous and lifelong process. Conversions proceed layer by layer, relationship by relationship, here a little, there a little—until the whole personality, intellect, feeling, and will have been recreated by God.[2]

A twenty-year-old college student came to see me in a crisis. After years of denial, she was finally facing the realization that she had been sexually abused as a child. That realization had landed her in a lot of pain and confusion. She told me that she had "turned it all over to Jesus" three weeks earlier. She'd asked him to heal her wounds, take away her pain, and resolve her torment. In a word, she wanted God to come with an eraser and make it go away. But God hadn't.

My eyes softened and I put my hand on hers, knowing too well the urgency she felt to have everything be okay again.

"If I can't trust God now, when I need him the most, how can I ever trust him again?" she cried. It wasn't a matter of whether God could be trusted, of course, but of whether or not she could wait. She didn't understand that there was a journey to be made here. A waiting, a gestating, a slow and uncertain birthing. *That* is where God was to be found. Not in the erasing of the experience, but in the embracing of it.

Archbishop William Temple once said that one of the mistakes Christians are fond of making is trying to be more spiritual than God. When Jesus was in pain, he didn't try to squirm out of it; rather, he embraced the pain. He let it happen. He experienced a sense of God's absence. He cried out, "My God, where are you? Why have you forsaken me?"

I tried to suggest to the college student before me that to be spiritual is to confront our pain, rather than make an enemy out of it. When Jesus told us to love our enemies, I suspect that he was talking about our inner enemies too. He knew that love was the only means by which to transform them.

I was part of a large group of people who gathered one fall at Kanuga Episcopal Conference Center in North Carolina. At the opening session we were each given a sheet of colored construction paper and asked to tear it into a shape that represented our life. We all got busy, creating lovely, colorful shapes. These were then collected and placed on a board to form one big collage. I thought our exercise had ended, but someone came around with a large glass bowl to collect the pieces of paper *we had torn away*—the refuse, the little scarred scraps we had intended to discard.

As the bowl with all the torn pieces was placed on the altar, it dawned on me what was happening. The bowl was symbolic of all our collective wounds—the confetti of scars and torn places we would like to be rid of. I was startled by the realization that it's only in gathering them up and embracing them, placing them on the altar, that we can begin the process of transforming them. Pain can be sacred too.

It's been hard for me to become brave enough to place my torn pieces in the bowl with everyone else's. I ran from the writing of this book for that very reason. Most of us Christians don't know how to wait in pain—at least not in the contemplative, creative way that opens us to newness and growth. We're told to "turn it over to Jesus" and—presto!—things should be okay.

But inside things usually aren't okay. So on top of everything else, we feel guilty because obviously we didn't *really* turn our pain over or else it wouldn't still be with us. Or we decide that God wasn't listening and can't be trusted to deliver on divine promises.

How did we ever get the idea that God would supply us on demand with quick fixes, that God is merely a rescuer and not a midwife?

BIBLICAL WAITING

Back home from my retreat at the monastery, I leafed through the Bible. If you want to be impressed, note how often God's people seem to be waiting. Noah waits for the flood waters to recede; Daniel waits through the night in a den of lions; Sarah waits in her barrenness for a child; Jacob waits for Rebecca's hand. The Israelites wait in Egypt, then wait forty more years in the desert. Later they wait seventy years in Babylonian captivity. Jonah waits in a fish's belly; Mary waits; Simeon waits to see the Messiah; the apostles wait for Pentecost; Paul waits in prison.

The Bible is rich with language urging us to wait. "For thee I wait all the day long" (Ps. 25:5). " My soul waits for the Lord more than watchmen for the morning" (Ps. 130:6). "Wait continually for your God" (Hos. 12:6). "If it seem slow, wait for it; it will surely come" (Hab. 2:3). "If we hope for what we do not see, we wait for it with patience" (Rom. 8:25).

[handwritten margin note: quotes from Bible re waiting x x x]

I came to the parable Jesus told about the ten maidens waiting for the bridegroom. Five came prepared with extra lamp oil to wait through the night. The other five didn't plan on having to wait, so they brought only the oil that was in their lamps. Naturally their lamps gave out. When they left to go buy more, the bridegroom showed up, and they missed him.

I'd always thought that the point of the story was that we should be prepared. But in my reading after the retreat, it seemed to be just as much about waiting. Waiting through the dark night. The idea is that waiting precedes celebration. If you don't show up prepared to wait, you may miss the transcendent when it happens.

Most stunning to me was the picture I began to get of *God* waiting. The parable of the prodigal son would be more aptly named the parable of the waiting father. It tells us much more about God than anything else—a God who watches and waits with a full heart for us to make our homecoming.

In rereading the stories of the Bible I glimpsed the portrait of a patient God who *enters into* the experience of those who wait. That portrait reminded me of the "gospel" story I'd read back in college about a lonely frightened porcupine named Joggi and a wounded raccoon named Gamiel.[3] As Gamiel waited to die and Joggi waited in his fears and loneliness, they created "a merciful being together."

It was an unusual partnership. Each creature was simply there with the other, no questions asked. Together they made a home— not a *place*, the story says, but a *bond*—a shelter of dwelling together in their pain, which made healing possible. That was what

I saw as I read the Scripture. I saw God making a home with us during our waiting, sharing the experience, no questions asked. Creating a "merciful being together."

ADDICTION TO THE QUICK AND EASY

Willingness to enter the "merciful being together" of waiting first of all means confronting how deep-seated our resistance to waiting really is. As I noted earlier, sometimes it seems we're becoming a nation of quickaholics—people compulsively seeking out quick and easy ways to live and solve problems, avoiding what is deep, difficult, and therefore growth-producing.

Anne Wilson Schaef maintains that "process addictions" occur when a person becomes hooked on a specific series of actions in order to avoid inner pain or inner growth. In her book *When Society Becomes an Addict*, she refers to watching television, running, accumulating money, and working, among other activities, as processes that can become addictive. She tells of a woman who made worry lists. This woman worried even when she felt good, because she was afraid the good feeling might go away. "When she didn't have anything specific to worry about, she felt lost and started to look for a 'worry fix.' . . . Worry had become an addictive process."[4]

I believe that in this same sense pursuing the quick and easy can become addictive; we avoid our lives by moving faster and faster, going from one shortcut to another. Obviously it isn't unhealthy to choose easier or less time-consuming ways to manage our lives. But when we begin to use these methods to avoid dealing with our inner condition—with problems, pain, and potential—we may cross the line.

I heard Marion Woodman, an expert in addictive behaviors, put it like this: The natural gradient in us is toward growth. Whatever we use repeatedly and compulsively to stop that growth is our particular addiction.

An addictive behavior "keeps us unaware of what is going on inside us," notes Schaef[5]. Darting through life at a progressively increasing speed diverts us from deeper realities. Likewise, latching onto easy, quick-fix solutions becomes a way of escaping the slow pain of uncertainty and self-confrontation. It helps us avoid the misery of wading through the inner mire toward change.

The quick and easy path is an "acceptable" way of avoidance, and one that can hold enormous power over us. We might complain (though that complaint is often hard to distinguish from boasting) of how pushed and hurried we feel, but we can't seem to extricate ourselves from the frenzy. We're unable to truly see that "there is more to life than increasing its speed," as Gandhi put it.

I talked with a highly successful businessman who's compulsively driven to quickness. The whole point of his life seemed to be to see how much he could do in the least amount of time. For him, the worst possible fate would be to wait. He had developed high blood pressure and other symptoms, and his doctor had advised him to slow down, or he was in for serious consequences.

As we talked, it became obvious how excruciating this idea of waiting really was. "Life is *moving*! If you don't want to be left behind, you keep moving too. I have to be doing something all the time," he cried, "I *have* to!"

"But why?" I asked him.

He looked at me—a little sadly, I think. "If I stop, I'll just end up thinking about my life," he said. "I think I'd rather die than have time on my hands." Addictions always lead us to death.

Like that businessman, I had to face the fact that my inability to wait was symptomatic of something amiss in my soul. I feared waiting because such pauses in life brought me close to the dark holes and empty pockets inside me, to the rigidities and self-lies I had fashioned.

Last year I met with a few of the monks of the Abbey of Gethsemani, the monastery where Merton had lived. As the conversation turned to waiting, Brother Anthony leaned forward in his chair. "Contemplative waiting is consenting to be where we really are," he explained. "People recoil from it because they don't want to be present to themselves. Such waiting causes a deep existential loneliness to surface, a feeling of being disconnected from oneself and God. At the depths there is fear, fear of the dark chaos within ourselves."

He had hit the heart of the addiction. We set up our obsessive patterns, pursuing the quick and easy, hurrying as fast as we can into the next moment, so that we don't have to dwell in this one. Brother Anthony was exactly right. Ultimately we're fleeing our own dark chaos. We're fleeing ourselves.

RULES OF THE QUICK AND EASY

As I confronted my own addictive tendencies to the quick and easy, I recognized in deeper ways how subtly our culture had fed my compulsions. I came upon three particular "rules" of modern life that seem to be at the heart of the problem.

All Lines Must Keep Moving

The next time you go into a bank or grocery store at a peak business hour, observe the people waiting. I showed up at my bank at a busy hour one day to find each of the four tellers' windows busy, with lines of seven and eight people at each. I let loose a sigh so loud that people turned to stare. My impulse was flight: I could leave and return at a less busy time. That would take more time in the long run, of course, but so what? At the moment, saving time wasn't the issue. What mattered was avoiding the misery of standing still.

I resigned myself, however. At that moment my fight response kicked in. I set my jaw, studying each line as if I were mapping out a military campaign. Which one would be the fastest? I picked the second line, because it was moving. The minute I got in it, however, the woman at the front stepped to the window with a bag full of quarters, nickels, dimes, and pennies for the teller to count. As we ground to a halt, everyone, including myself, muttered and fumed.

The man in front of me shifted from one foot to the other. A little collar of perspiration had formed around his neck. He switched to another line. A moment later the line he'd deserted began to move, and his new line stopped. He was so put out that he left the bank in a huff.

We were a bank full of quickaholics.

Disney World in Florida is sensitive to America's extreme resistance to waiting. I heard a Disney employee explain that the lines to the attractions were looped and snaked to give the feeling of movement. The worst thing, he pointed out, is to let the crowd stand still. "All lines must keep moving," he said. "That's rule number one." The secret is to divert people so that they don't realize how miserable they are standing there waiting.

All lines must keep moving. That's one of the primary rules of modernity. Movement is a kind of diversion from our inner misery. Without the stimulation of forward motion, we're troubled by thoughts we usually keep at bay. Yet stillness is essential, as Alan Jones points out:

> Poor Alice in *Through the Looking Glass* has to run furiously in order to stay in the same place. We, on the other hand, have to learn to stand still in order to continue our journey. We must stand still.... The more we run around, the more we lose touch with ourselves, the less of us there is.... The still journey of the soul takes forever.[6]

Overcoming my resistance to waiting meant coming to terms with the "still journey." I would have to give up the compulsion to keep my line moving at the world's pace. I would need to find my own pace, one that flowed with the rhythms of the earth and the Spirit, not with the frenzy of modern life.

Our inner clocks tick at a much slower speed than that of society. Slowing our feet, our minds, our desires, our impulses—stilling those things that drive us into faster and faster patterns of living—will help open us to the transforming experience of waiting.

Counselor Helen Luke cautions that without significant times to be still, we "extinguish the possibility of growth and walk backwards."[7] Here's the paradox: we achieve our deepest progress standing still.

G. K. Chesterton reportedly said that in Christianity we don't have *doxology* so much as we have *paradoxology*. And here's one of the trickiest of paradoxes: when we keep the line moving forward at the expense of inward motion, something deep within us "walks backwards."

That paradox, and the image of walking backwards, whirled my mind once again to the the story of the two caterpillars, Stripe and Yellow. Before spinning their cocoons, they spent all their time (as did all the other caterpillars), climbing up a great column of "squirming, pushing caterpillars—a caterpillar pillar." The point seemed to be to reach the top. No one knew what was up there. They only hoped that the summit would offer them what they were looking for in life. But their existence was pretty frantic, with lots of rushing and straining. It boiled down to climb or be climbed.

Finally, disenchanted with crawling up, Stripe and Yellow became still. Soon they were at the bottom of the pile, free to spin the cocoons that would give them wings. To their delight, they found that wings were the only way to get to the top. Thus Stripe and Yellow made their deepest progress standing still.

I was learning that being still and waiting in one place—going not forward but inward—was the sort of progress that really counted, the sort that gave us wings.

For years I had prayed for a mentor, for someone to whom I could turn now and then for wisdom and guidance. About a year before finding my February cocoon, I encountered the writings of Dr. Beatrice Bruteau; and I had no doubt that she was that mentor. I arranged to meet her, expecting a tall woman, a big presence. What I found was a short, slight woman with a big presence. A retired professor of philosophy, a brilliant scholar, and a spiritual voyager, she mentored and I soaked up. She has taught me a lot.

Struggling now with how to remain in my cocoon, I turned to her for guidance. As we visited one morning in her kitchen in North Carolina, she turned her bright, snapping eyes on me. "Sue, do you know what *entrainment* is?" she asked.

I shook my head.

"It's the phenomenon of two rhythmic beings gradually altering their movements until they're moving together in the same rhythm. Pendulums hanging on the same wall do it; crickets do it when they chirp; even people do it when they talk. The point is we tend to align ourselves with the rhythm and pace around us. If you want to stay in your waiting, you'll need to refrain from the frantic pace around you. The important thing is to be still."

Her advice is far from that of the amusement park official who said that the most important thing is to keep moving. Keep moving. Be still. Here are the two diverging paths: one that urges us out of our waiting and one that takes us into the contemplative heart of it.

One of the best known but least observed verses in the Bible is this: "Be still, and know that I am God" (Ps. 46:10, KJV). The verse tells us something so powerful that we scarcely recognize it. It informs us that in the act of being still there's a knowing, a transcendent knowing that's available to us at no other time.

The dizzy pace at which we travel can be destructive not just for individual hearts but for the whole planet. Our hasty forward progress has created acid rain, toxic waste, and other frightening realities that are destroying our environment. It has created weapons systems with increasingly destructive capabilities. We're moving so rapidly there hasn't been enough time to ponder and reflect spiritually, psychologically, or philosophically on what we're creating. We desperately need waiting time as a society to confront what we're doing.

God seems to be calling us to the experience of waiting not only individually but collectively, as a world family. That doesn't mean that God calls us away from progress, but to progress aged with deep spiritual reflection. For a world that hovers so delicately between beauty and destruction, waiting is something we can't afford to ignore much longer.

Make Life Happen

Another "rule" of life that fosters our resistance to waiting is the notion that we must *make* life happen rather than simply *let* life happen.

There was a time when I envisioned waiting as having the hold button on my life pushed momentarily; I was disengaged from life. Time stopped—or worse, it continued while I sat there passively holding the receiver. This vision grew out of my bias that life doesn't "happen" while you wait. It happens only when you're out there engaged with peak events, when you're doing things, when you're making a big agenda for life.

Mostly I saw life "happening" in the future. It can be jolting to discover how much of life we project there. When I was a child, life revolved around waiting for school to end each day, for summer vacation to arrive, for birthdays and Christmas. As a teenager I waited for my first date, my driver's license, my high school and college graduation. I waited to get married, to have children, to start a career. I waited for my career to grow. The tendency is to see that waiting time as a wasteland of minutes, hours, and days all heaped up like junked cars.

We think that the "real thing" is concentrated in the *next* moment, the *next* month, the *next* year. We can go on and on, waiting for the next "happening" of life, hurrying toward it, trying to make it happen. We live from peak event to peak event, from brightness to brightness, resisting the flat terrain of ordinary time—the in-between time.

Waiting is the in-between time. It calls us to be in this moment, this season, without leaning so far into the future that we tear our roots from the present. When we learn to wait, we experience where we are as what is truly substantial and precious in life. We discover, as T. S. Eliot wrote, "a lifetime burning in every moment."[8]

When I deliberately carved out a time of waiting and entered my cocoon, I had to struggle to let life happen rather than thinking I must constantly make it happen. I had to turn myself loose and trust that life could take place with fullness and grace right now, even though I was firm (and even active) in my nondoing.

This particular stance is hard to describe, much less experience. It's captured in what the Chinese call *wu wei*. This is an attitude of expectant beingness—a nondoing or actionless action that Thomas Merton said "is not intent upon results and is not concerned with consciously laid plans or deliberately organized endeavors."[9] *Wu wei* is the opposite of conquest or conscious striving. Merton compared it to St. Paul's teachings on spiritual liberty—that is, coming at life from a basic standpoint of faith and freedom, not achieving and straining. We simply let life unfold.

Wu wei is based on the idea that God makes available inside us all that we need to grow and become whole; Jesus himself referred to this truth when he spoke of the kingdom of God as a self-sowing seed. It's "as if a man should scatter seed upon the ground, and should sleep and rise night and day, and the seed should sprout and grow, he knows not how. The earth produces of itself, first the blade, then the ear, then the full grain" (Mark 4:26–28).

I love those little-explored words of Jesus. They tell me that the hidden potential and fullness of life is within me. My part is to wait in creative and expectant ways for it to unfold, attentive to the process.

Farmers are usually good at grasping Jesus' concept of the self-sowing seed. They know that the flower is contained in the seed. Everything is present there. One can only wait and watch and be present to it as it blossoms.

This is an important principle in waiting: coming to the enormous realization that there are seed forces within us. The potential for wholeness, Life with a capital L, is fully here. We don't have to go out in conquest and make it happen. We can simply let it happen, *consciously.*

My grandfather was a lawyer, a judge, and a farmer. He was frequently busy and conquesting, but I remember also that he sometimes entered into golden moments of *wu wei.* He and I used to go fishing at one of the little ponds on his farm. He would sit and hold his cane pole over the water, becoming as still as the stumps that jutted up from the water. I usually tired of fishing fairly soon and went on to other things, like dandelions. One day having given up on the fishing, I was playing in his old black truck when I noticed that his fishing bait was still on the seat. I remember being surprised that my grandfather had been out fishing an hour or more without bait.

I grabbed the bait basket and raced over to him. "Grandaddy, how can you fish without bait?"

He tilted back his hat and smiled as if he had been caught in some delicious secret. "Well, sometimes it's not the fish I'm after, " he said, "it's the fishing."

In other words, it wasn't the conquest that mattered, but being in the moment, fully in the experience, watching and waiting as life unfolded. He was letting life happen.

Of course, letting life happen doesn't mean that we resort to futile resignation. It doesn't mean that we don't have goals and aspirations for the future; rather, it means giving up our need to manipulate and control, to "bait" all the events and minutes around us. We can relax and relate to life with a faithful knowing that if we cease to act, life itself will not cease. It may, in fact, grow full.

Jung expressed it like this: "The art of letting things happen, action through non-action,. . .became for me the key opening the door to the way. We must be able to let things happen in the psyche. For us, this actually is an art of which few people know anything."[10]

Meister Eckhart, the mystic whose fourteenth-century writings are full of dazzling insights for our era, also wrote about letting life happen. He called it being in "true poverty."[11] Emptied of the need to achieve, a person could be free to wait in the moment. It was, he conceded, the highest way of being.

Eckhart believed that in learning this way of being we would begin to experience God as the "newest" thing there is. In waiting we find (perhaps for the first time) God new and immediate in every moment, not something "out there" to be grasped some other time.

Eat Dessert First

If you want a hint of what's going on in the American soul, take a look at the things printed on people's T-shirts. I saw one recently that said, "Life is uncertain. . .so eat dessert first."

I have to confess that I smiled. It reminded me of the time my son, then small, begged to eat his chocolate pie before his broccoli. "No! Broccoli first, dessert last," I ordered. This was the simple order of the universe: unpleasant first, pleasant last.

I left him staring at his plate. When I returned, the broccoli was gone and he was starting on pie. Weeks later I traced an incredibly foul smell to his closet. There I found a heap of rotten broccoli in his Tonka dumptruck. He had found a way to circumvent the painful task of eating his vegetables. He got the result he desired the quick and easy way. Of course, there's almost always a bad smell attached to such behavior.

The slogan "Life is uncertain. . .so eat dessert first" is another rule of life that undermines our waiting. It taunts us with an approach to life that's rampant in our culture: when life gets unpredictable, skip the unpleasant and tedious and go for instant gratification. Forget broccoli; cut right to the pie.

Psychiatrist Scott Peck writes, "Delaying gratification is a process of scheduling the pain and pleasure of life in such way as to enhance the pleasure by meeting and experiencing the pain first and getting it over with. It is the only decent way to live."[12]

To cultivate the discipline of delayed gratification we have to learn one elemental thing, to face pain. Ultimately, we covet what's fast and instant because we don't want to endure the suffering of going the long way round.

I found that seeking to avoid legitimate difficulty and going for instant satisfaction was one of the more treacherous obstacles on my waiting journey. One day, when I thought I could endure waiting no longer, I confided to my counselor, "I can't go on with this. I'd rather do *something*, even if it's disastrous, than continue to wait."

"The pain won't kill you," he said, "but running from it might." Here was one of the more valuable lessons I learned: avoiding pain, rather than having the discipline and courage to confront it and live it through, only compounds suffering in the long run. The escape hatches people create in attempts to avoid or numb pain can actually be worse than the experience of pain they sought to avoid in the first place. As Helen Luke notes, "As long as we seek to escape from our various 'hells' into freedom from pain, we remain irremediably bound; we can emerge from the pains of Hell in one way only—by accepting another kind of suffering, the suffering which is purging."[13]

Recently a friend and I sat in a corner booth having lunch. Neither of us was very hungry. She had just finished telling me that her marriage of eighteen years was ending. Her agony was great and piercing.

"Are you sure there's no hope?" I asked.

"I don't know if there's hope," she said. "I only know that I can't stick around to find out. The pain of waiting it out would be too awful. I'd rather just do it, and put it behind me."

There was a long and awful pause while I groped for something to say. Nothing came. She started to cry; then I started to cry. "Oh, Sue, do you know what it's like to feel such pain that you would do *anything*, give up *anything* to be out of it?"

I drew in my breath. I saw myself walking through that aching winter abyss, my secure life crumbling, things in disarray, so lost in pain. I remembered how I wanted to be out of it all, how I begged for relief and came instead upon the cocoon in the tree.

"I've had my moments," I told her.

"And what did you do?"

I hesitated, aware that my answer might not be hers. "I waited," I finally said.

"Was it worth it—the waiting, I mean?"

"It was worth it," I answered her.

The point of waiting wasn't necessarily to give her a reconciled marriage but to offer her a way for transformation of her own self, a way to give birth to something new and beautiful in her soul.

YEASTING

That's the kind of winter it became as I wrestled to unravel the cultural myths and fast-fix spirituality that eroded my ability to wait in God. It was a time of "undoing" the rules that had rocketed me into pursuit of the quick and easy. Slowly I began to trust the solitary voice in me that said that standing still meant forward progress, that letting life happen rather than striving to make it happen allowed life to unfold with even more beauty and potential, that facing pain wasn't nearly so terrible as avoiding it.

Whenever you undo a false pattern of believing, God seems to come with fresh insights and images that unleash new energy and enable you to move ahead. For me, faith was believing that the God who whirled the darkness in me would also create the radiance. So I waited.

One Wednesday morning in March I went for Communion at the Espicopal church where I have been confirmed as a member. As I arrived at the altar to receive the bread, I noticed that the place on the cushion where I was about to kneel was embroidered with a butterfly. I knelt upon it as if I was sinking upon a promise, a promise of healing and fullness of being, of creation and life. After the bread was placed in my palm, I stared at it a long while before lifting it to my lips. Bread of life, I kept thinking.

That evening I curled up in my blue wing chair with my sketch pad and drew a simple loaf of homebaked bread. I drew it tall and full on a cutting board beside a kitchen knife.

It pulled up a memory inside me. . . .

My daughter, who was then five, pulled a kitchen chair to the counter where I was baking bread. You might as well know that I don't normally bake bread. In fact, I had never baked a loaf of bread before and haven't baked a loaf since. But that day my creative instinct was popping out not in the usual way but in an unpremeditated attack of domesticity. I had wanted to make something from nothing, from scratch, something that would nourish people.

Ann was fascinated. She knelt on the chair, her face powdered with self-rising flour, and watched my every move. When we got to the part where you put in the yeast and cover the dough so that it will rise, I put a blue-checkered dishcloth over the bowl the way my mother used to do and set it aside.

Ann wrinkled her brow. "Aren't you going to finish?" she asked.

"We have to wait for the dough to rise," I told her. I explained how the yeast causes the dough to expand.

"Well, how long do we have to wait?" she asked.

I looked at the recipe. "An hour."

"A *whole* hour?" She grimaced and plopped down in her chair to wait it out. Now and then her impatience overflowed and she lifted the cloth to peek at the dough. "It's not doing anything," she announced.

"You can't see it, but the yeast is working. I promise."

I don't think she believed me. She finally wandered off to play.

Toward the end of the hour, though, she returned to peer into the bowl. Her face lit up. "Look, Mama, it's yeasting!" she proclaimed.

Yeasting. As the memory faded, that word stayed with me. Yeasting. I looked at the sketch in my lap and felt the promise rise beneath me. Isn't that the invisible mystery inside our waiting which produces the bread of life?

To create newness you have to cover the soul and let grace rise. You must come to the place where there's nothing to do but brood, as God brooded over the deep, and pray and be still and trust that the holiness that ferments the galaxies is working in you too. Only wait.

And somehow the transformation you knew would never come, that impossible plumping of fresh life and revelation, *does* come. It manifests itself in unseen slowness. So it would happen to me and so it will happen to all who set out to knead their pain and wounds, their hopes and hungers, into bread. Waiting is the yeasting of the human soul.

Jungian analyst James Hillman says that our "soul is the patient part of us."[14] Only as we go inward and get in touch with it will we be able to authentically wait.

Yet if we *choose* a time of waiting, our extroverted society will do its best to pull us away. We may be called selfish and lazy, too introspective, self-indulgent. "What are you waiting for? Get up and *do* something. Take action." When such voices came, I tried to remember the small voice of my daughter, calling me to the depth and solitude of myself, to the experience of patient yeasting.

In the end, God and I would make bread.

CHAPTER 3

From False Self to True Self

Who in the world am I? Ah, that's the great puzzle.

LEWIS CARROLL

Jesus then asked him, "What is your name?" And he said, "Legion."

LUKE 8:30

The shell must be cracked apart if what is in it is to come out, for if you want the kernel, you must break the shell.

MEISTER ECKHART

In March my thoughts turned more and more to the transformation that takes place within the waiting heart. What are the changes and growth I am being asked to undergo? What is the movement that is happening inside of me, and where do I begin?

WAITING SONG

These questions were on my mind one warm March evening as I sat on my daughter's bed, braiding her hair into an intricate silky cord. Earlier she'd been teaching me her dance steps for the spring recital. We'd held hands, twirling gracefully around her bedroom, dancing to the rise and fall of our own laughing. Now we were silent as I wove her hair back and forth through my fingers.

Suddenly the wind chimes began to play a song from the patio. *Ting, ting, ting.* "What's that, Mama?" she asked.

"Let's go see," I suggested. As we walked outside, I held onto her hair, afraid that all my efforts at braiding would unravel.

Purple shadows criss-crossed the garden. In the twilight four new daffodils were swaying in the breeze, moving with the melody of the chimes. I thought back to the December day I'd laid the bulbs in the earth, leaving them to wait. A novice in the garden, I'd buried the bulbs nearly a foot deep. "Good grief! A few inches would have been sufficient," a gardener friend told me later. Knowing that, I had wondered whether the daffodils would even come up. But here they were, nodding at me.

As Ann and I gazed at them, I was struck by how extraordinary their feat really was—those delicate shoots breaking through the soil, through all the darkness I'd heaped on them. I wondered if that was the same mystery going on in the soil of my own life. Was there a truer, more whole self buried in me under layers of heaped darkness? Was I being asked to break through the layers of my false selves and let the True Self emerge?

The sound floated again through the dusk. *Ting. Ting. Ting.* "What is that, Mama?" Ann repeated. I smiled. I wanted to tell my daughter that it was more than she could ever imagine, this sound. It wasn't just wind striking the chimes under the eaves. It was a waiting song, a song about what is deep and holy pressing to the light.

"Show me the dance for the spring recital one more time," I said to her. I turned loose her hair and let all the weaving fall free. She took my hands and we spun round the purple edges of the garden, moving with the daffodils to the waiting song.

That night, when I kissed Ann goodnight, she said, "Mama, I liked that dance."

"Me too," I said. All night I could scarcely sleep. I kept hearing the soft tinging in the air.

THE TRUE SEED

Over and over again God calls you and me to the gardening of our own divine depths, to the cultivation of what Meister Eckhart called the "true seed" within us. God calls us to tend what lies seeded in the soul, this kernel of our truest nature—the God-image or True Self.

Eckhart identified the true seed as the living presence of God's image implanted in the soul. "There is something in the soul which is only God," he wrote.[1] I can't think of anything that creates such a a feeling of awe in me.

He wasn't saying that the soul *is* God, but that God is *in* the soul, that the soul is the holy soil in which the divine life of God is planted for us to cultivate and experience. He wrote, "God has sowed his image....He sows the seed of the divine nature....The seed of God is in us. If the seed had a good, wise and industrious cultivator, it would thrive and grow up into God. "[2]

Could it be that at the most fundamental level this is what it means to grow spiritually? Could it be that this is the meaning of the verse, "We are to grow up in every way into...Christ" (Eph. 4:15)?

After that March evening I began to get a new glimpse of the process of spiritual transformation: there's a bulb of truth buried in the human soul that's "only God"—God's image and likeness. Throughout our lives we create patterns of living that obscure this identity. We heap on the darkness, constructing a variety of false selves. We become adept at playing games, wearing masks as if life were a masquerade party. This can go on for a long while. But eventually the music of the True Self seeks us out. Sooner or later (often in midlife), we're summoned back to the garden. We're called to soul-work.

About this time I discovered Hildegard of Bingen, a woman of the twelfth century who was an extraordinary preacher, theologian, doctor, scientist, artist, composer, and writer. She was a towering spiritual presence, all but forgotten now. Recently my daughter was watching a beauty contest on television. When the host asked the finalists which female figure in history they would most like to spend an evening with, answers ran from Marilyn Monroe to Betsy Ross. Ann asked who my choice would be. "Hildegard of Bingen," I said, almost without thinking. When I tried to explain who she was, Ann rolled her eyes to the ceiling in exasperation. "You come up with some dingers," she said.

I grinned, for it was true that Hildegard rang a clear, holy bell in me. She said that the soul was like a precious field from which we must "root out the useless grasses, thorns, and briars" in order to reveal the beauty of God's image glistening in the soil. To Hildegard, sin was failing to care for the soul, failing to water it and give it what she called "greening power." The saddest thing, to Hildegard, was a "drooping soul."[3]

I began to get an almost stunning sense of how little attention we Christians have paid to the soul as the seedbed of divine life within us. We've mostly looked at it as something to *save*—an immortal essence in need of redeeming. How many souls have you won? then becomes the central question of Christian life. But the soul is more than something to win or save. It's the seat and repository of the inner Divine, the God-image, the truest part of us.

I woke fresh to the knowledge that the soul is the place where we meet God. "Here God's ground is my ground and my ground is God's ground," Eckhart wrote.[4] When I began to see the soul in this light, the important thing became not saving the soul but entering it, greening it, developing the divine seed that waits realization. I realized that the heart of religion was setting up an honest dialogue with the uniqueness of one's soul and finding a deeply personal relationship with God, the inner Voice, the inner Music that plays in you as it does in no one else.

I'm aware that, if it stopped there, religion would be in danger of becoming inward and selfish. That's why Eckhart and Hildegard both insisted that the discovery and tending of the true seed must expand into compassion. As the seed branches out, one's soul intertwines with others in loving, reconciling ways.

But the question here is whether we've been so busy saving souls that we've neglected the unfolding of the God-image within them. Have we suppressed our souls, imprisoning the True Self under layers of falseness, wounding, conformity, and even conventional religious practice? Is Christianity becoming a sanctum of drooping souls?

During those early spring days, as I contemplated the daffodil bulbs and the "true seed," I turned a corner in my waiting journey. I began to sense God calling me to the primary spiritual experience of soulmaking. It was as if God were whispering to me, The soul wants to be acknowledged and nurtured. The True Self wants to bloom and grow. And the way to begin this spiritual flowering is to confront your false selves—the ego patterns you have created—and come home to who you really are inside.

WHITTLING AWAY

There's an old Carolina story I like about a country boy who had a great talent for carving beautiful dogs out of wood. Every day he sat on his porch whittling, letting the shavings fall around him. One day a visitor, greatly impressed, asked him the secret of his art. "I just take a block of wood and whittle off the parts that don't look like a dog," he replied.

In down-home language, this anecdote describes the movement of growth I'm referring to. The art of soulmaking is taking our lives in our hands and—with all the love and discernment we can muster—gently whittling away the parts that don't resemble the True Self. In spiritual whittling, though, we don't discard the shavings. Transformation happens not by rejecting these parts of ourselves but by gathering them up and integrating them. Through this process we reach a new wholeness.

Spiritual whittling is an encounter with Mystery, waiting, the silence of inner places—all those things most folks no longer have time for. I'll be honest. As I began my own spiritual whittling, I often clung to my "block of wood" resistantly. After all, wasn't I fine just as I was? Why should I embrace an art that could demand so much patience and be so difficult?

But there were also days when I felt drawn to try, when I yearned to discover how I was living falsely. At times it even seemed that I was pulled into a winding Pied Piper journey I couldn't help but follow, because not to meant missing the most irresistible adventure of all: becoming real.

The writings of Thomas Merton encouraged me. He envisioned much of the spiritual life as whittling away the false self in order to become the True Self. He called the struggle for authenticity a "contemplative crisis" and insisted that no one can avoid it, that eventually we all "get the treatment." According to Merton, "One's actual self may be far from 'real,' since it may be profoundly alienated from one's own deep spiritual identity. To reach one's 'real self' one must, in fact, be delivered from that illusory and false 'self' whom we have created."[5]

How real am I, I asked myself. What are the illusions I've created? What false selves do I need to pare away? Those are the whittling questions. Taken seriously, they're tough and agonizing. "We are not very good at recognizing illusions, least of all the ones we cherish about ourselves," wrote Merton.[6]

Gradually I took time to probe and reflect. Bit by bit I encountered patterns of falseness, wounds, and cherished illusions that came together to form false selves.

THE SELF WITH A CAPITAL S

As I struggled to confront these selves (which I describe later in this chapter), I found valuable insights in the work of C. G. Jung. I want to pass on one or two or them because Jung's vision offers us Christians a viable, revitalizing way of seeing our own lifelong process of spiritual becoming.

Jung demonstrated that there's a True Self dimension of the human personality; he called this the Self with a capital S. It has been called his most profound and far-reaching discovery. *Self* is an unfortunate name, though, because it tends to mislead people. *Self* doesn't refer to our narrow identity or our ego (as in my*self*) but to the Center, the image of God within us. It's been compared to the inner kingdom that Jesus referred to (Luke 17:21).

If that isn't exciting enough, Jung also believed that the foremost drive within the human is toward wholeness and realization of the Self. Along with Hildegard and Eckhart, he believed that we have an inborn tendency to uncover the God-image within us.

We can think of the Self as already within us, an imprint of wholeness and divinity that's fully encompassing, but we must also see it as (to borrow Episcopal priest and Jungian analyst John Sanford's words) a "potentiality striving to become realized in us."[7] I sometimes think of the True Self as a bulb buried in the dark ground of my unconscious, seeking to push into the conscious light above. You've perhaps noticed how window plants wind and grow toward the light, pressing their leaves against the pane. This turning toward the sun has a scientific name; it's called *heliotropism*. Jung spoke of a "human heliotropism." The True Self seeks the light, winding and growing toward realization, pressing against the window pane of consciousness.

I can't tell you how this tiny glimpse of Jung's psychology widened, deepened, and affirmed my spiritual journeying. Jung called this path toward wholeness in which the Self seeks realization "individuation," since it means becoming a unique and completed individual—the person God created us to be. The question that began to resonate inside me was this: What would it mean for me to step onto the path of individuation? Where would I end up? I only knew in the depths of me that it was a holy, God-saturated path.

THE EGOCENTRIC EGO

I also grew aware of another center in the human psyche: the self with a lower case *s*, or the ego. To understand our false selves, we need to look closely at this dimension of ourselves.

The ego is the part of us with which we identify. It's "the executive of the conscious personality," writes John Sanford.[8] A strong ego, aware of its boundaries, is crucial to wholeness and healthy functioning. In fact, the ego is like the window pane of consciousness toward which the True Self grows and expresses itself in one's life. We can't do without it.

The problem arises when the ego becomes egocentric, an unavoidable human condition. As we attempt to adapt to and protect ourselves from the wounds and realities of life, we each create a unique variety of defense structures—patterns of thinking, behaving, and relating designed to protect the ego. *These egocentric patterns make up our false selves.*

Throughout life these ego structures progressively harden, darkening the pane and thereby cutting the ego off from the Self. As a result, that vital connection with the True Self cannot be fully made. Jesus referred to this condition as hardness of heart (Mark 8:17).

The spiritual journey entails confronting these hardened patterns that we've spent a lifetime creating, patterns that oppose the life of the spirit and obscure our true spiritual identity. Overcoming them means allowing God to transform even our most prized illusions about ourselves.

As this inner picture of what happens deep inside us came together for me, I realized that a major pitfall of human life was believing that these rigid ego patterns or masks are who we really are, that there's nothing beyond the ingrained patterns we live out every day. Is that what I had done? Had my masks gotten stuck to my face? Were facets of me living the cramped life of the ego, alienated from the wider, richer life of the Self?

When these insights began to sink in (and it took some time for that to happen), I began to see how my own spiritual stage had been set for this great and universal drama, a drama on which the curtain frequently rises at midlife. It was a drama in which the false selves of the ego and the true identity of the Self wrestle for primacy in the human personality.

The truth that I had begun to discover that evening in the soft light of the March garden was being affirmed to me: in order for the ego to relinquish its central position, my hardened structures must be cracked open. This process opens a way for the gradual shift of centers, a deep restructuring away from the ruling needs of the ego toward the Self, or the core of God within.

In Christian language, this is plain, old-fashioned surrender—giving up our conscious will and striving, and yielding instead to the inner kingdom.

The soul-work involved in this internal restructuring is, I believe, the deepest meaning of spiritual becoming.

NOT I, BUT CHRIST

These ideas were a great puzzle for me. How did they weave together with the Scripture? One night, as I sat up late reading in the Epistles, I saw more clearly how Christianity teaches that we have a True Self—a "mind of Christ" (1 Cor. 2:16), an indwelling Christ (Col. 1:27, Phil. 1:21, Rom. 8:9–10), an inner Christ-self that's unformed and unfinished (Eph. 4:13, 15).

As I read Galatians 2:20—"It is no longer I who live, but Christ who lives in me"—I wondered, Could *this* be the sacred process of becoming a true individual and discovering the ground of I AM in one's own soul? Is discovering and developing the "mind of Christ" the bending, curving journey toward the light?

I closed the Bible, feeling the deep click of truth that comes when God reaches out in startling ways from its pages. We seem to think that God speaks by seconding the ideas we've already adopted, but God nearly always catches us by surprise. If it's God's Spirit blowing, someone ends up having feathers ruffled in an unforeseen way. God tends to confound, astonish, and flabbergast. A Bethlehem stable, a Roman cross, an empty garden tomb. We might as well reconcile ourselves to the fact that God's truth often turns up in ways we don't expect.

Referring to the verse I just quoted from Galatians, John Sanford writes,

> In this statement Paul tells us that his personality has been reorganized in such a way that it no longer revolves around his Ego, but around a larger center within himself that he calls the Christ within. This is the essential thought…that in the course of our lifetime our personalities are to be transformed and reorganized in such a way that the Ego, with its ambitions and goals, is no longer the main reference point.[9]

Through that statement I began to feel a convergence of all these varied thoughts—from Eckhart and Hildegard to Merton to Jung to Paul—that moved me at a deep level. With these insights casting new light on Scripture, I began to see the midlife soulscape in sharper focus. The words, "not I, but Christ" urged me to come home to myself more fully, to the petaled truth buried deep within.

NIGHT PRAYER

One night I put my reading aside and walked outside under the stars to sit on the grass. There's something about a vast night sky full of blazing stars that spins life back into proportion and soothes the frayed and hurting places in me. St. Teresa pointed out that the door of entry to the soul is prayer and reflection.[10] Night prayers, more than any others, seem to carry us over the portal. A night prayer is one said against a backdrop of darkness or beneath the shadow of pain. It's in those circumstances that we most often find the honest feelings and searing words that can plunge us into change.

I opened my journal; and by the spill of light from the porch, the moon, and the stars, a prayer—a night prayer of both darkness and pain—came pouring from my heart. I wrote it down, hardly knowing what I was about to unleash in my life:

God, I don't want to live falsely, in self-imposed prisons and fixed, comfortable patterns that confine my soul and diminish the truth in me. So much of me has gone underground. I want to let my soul out. I want to be free to risk what's true, to be myself. Set free the daring in me—the willingness to go within, to see the self-lies. I'll try to run away, but don't let me. Don't let me stifle myself with prudence that binds the creative revisioning of life and the journey toward wholeness.

I'm scared, God. Make me brave. Lead me into the enormous spaces of becoming. Help me cease the small, tedious work of maintaining and protecting so that I can break the masks that obscure your face shining in the night of my own soul. Help me to green my soul and risk becoming the person you created me to be.

Tomorrow I may regret these words, but tonight I speak them, for I know that you're somewhere inside them, that you love me and won't leave me alone in their echo.

I shut my journal and stared at the web of stars overhead. I wondered if this was how beginnings were made—in the momentary flarings of a scared but burning heart.

THE COLLECTIVE "THEY"

Change begins with the recognition that we're not so much an "I" as a "they." We may like to think that we're individuals living out our own unique truth, but more often we're scripts written collectively by society, family, church, job, friends, and traditions. Sometimes our life becomes a matter of simply playing the various roles for which we've been scripted...playing them out perfectly, in the right sequence, in full costume and mask.

Author Linda Leonard reminds us that "in trying to adapt to an image from outside projected by parents and society, we become reduced to an object, to an It. Our lives become mundane and banal, we become fascinated by trivial matters and mystery is lost—the mystery of our unique selves."[11]

We need our outer roles and identities, of course, but we also need to live them *authentically*, in ways that are true to our unique and inner self. When we live exclusively out of the expectations thrust on us from without, rather than living from the truth emerging within, we become caught in the collective "they."

I asked myself repeatedly, over the course of days and weeks, what seemed like the silliest question: Okay, Sue Monk Kidd, who are you? And I always heard the obvious answer: "I'm Sandy's wife, Bob and Ann's mother, Leah and Ridley's daughter, a church member, a writer, a..."

One day, as I drove to the post office, that little dialogue started up in my head. A pressing question broke right into the middle of my rote response: So if all those roles were suddenly stripped away, what would be left? Who would you be then?

Now there's a menacing question: Who *would* I be? The question sliced through the obvious, and suddenly I felt as if I were looking in a mirror at my original face, hearing my real name called for the first time.

As I parked the car at the post office, tears began pouring down my face. I am, I thought. *That's all.* I was shocked by wonder at this unbidden and penetrating "knowing" of who I was. Inside I felt reshuffled, revisioned, widened, breathed into.

I look back at that experience with a smile. I mean, there I was, sitting in a parking space at the U.S. post office having an ontological experience, an experience of pure beingness. But that's how such splinterings of God often pierce us. In an unsuspecting moment the scales fall off our eyes, the optical illusions vanish, and we're standing before what Rudolph Otto called "the *mysterium tremendum*"—the bare mystery of simply being. (I never did buy stamps that day.)

We need to allow that question. As a matter of fact, lots of times we need questions more than answers. Questions such as these: Is there more to me than the roles I live out? Can I open up to my identity apart from them, to the knowledge that I'm more than the personas I create?

Philosopher Sören Kierkegaard wrote that the "ultimate thing" is "whether you yourself are conscious of that most intimate relation to yourself as an individual."[12] This "ultimate" recognition is a necessary part of growing up.

One day, crossing the street, I noticed a bumper sticker on a car that said, "I refuse to grow up." In the spiritual life this is a deadly motto to follow. I looked through the car's window at the driver, an adult woman. She looked safe and comfortable, and with a shock I recognized myself. A lot of days I didn't want to grow up either.

"At some point, if we are to continue to grow, we must begin to differentiate ourselves from the roles we play. Often we do this when the roles that felt good initially now feel empty," notes author

Carol Pearson.[13] A lot of my roles were feeling empty. Slowly, as I probed my life, I began to see how much of me was embedded in the collective "they," how I tended to live out the scripting and expectations thrust on me rather than my own truth.

Author Sam Keen calls the appearance of the True Self from beneath roles the emergence of the "outlaw."[14] A daunting name, isn't it? It's used in the sense that one is growing beyond the confining "laws" imposed from without or from one's history. He describes the outlaw quest not as rebellion but as a crucial stage of healthy inner growth in which the adult tills up the myths, masks, and ego defenses that were constructed during the first half of life. It's the first movement away from the herd instinct toward the True Self, a struggle to pull oneself from the powerful suction of the collective "they" and become an authentic "I."

NAMING FALSE SELVES

In the weeks that followed I began a process of "naming" my false selves, a process that spanned many weeks of looking within and reflecting on my life. By naming the inner patterns that imprison us, we come to know them more fully and obtain a certain power over them. God told Adam to name the animals as part of the process of obtaining "dominion over them" (Gen. 2:19). My false selves—these encrustations of my own weak and wounded ego—are not so particular to me. In sharing them with others, I've found that we human beings are more alike than different. In the "humus" of our soul, we find common soil, common seed, the same heaped darkness.

Nevertheless, our task is to dip our hands into the soil of our own lives and name the patterns unique to us. The patterns that follow aren't meant to be comprehensive; neither are they categories into which we neatly fit. We may reflect various aspects of these profiles at different times, in different situations. They're offered as windows through which you might catch a glimpse or two of yourself.

Little Girl with a Curl

A picture that hung on the wall over my bed when I was a child came to live on a wall inside me. It was of a black-haired little girl dressed in a delicate blue dress. She held a parasol and smiled a sweet, docile smile. It was often said that she bore a resemblance to me.

What fascinated me most about her was one black curl that dangled down into the middle of her forehead, a straying curl that had a mind of its own. I had one of those curls myself.

Whenever I looked at the little girl with the charming smile and straying curl who presided over my room, I thought of the nursery rhyme my parents often quoted to me:

> There was a little girl who had a little curl,
> Right in the middle of her forehead.
> When she was good, she was very very good.
> When she was bad she was horrid.

My parents' voices soared happily when they recited the part about the girl's goodness and sank when they came to her horridness. That was, after all, part of the drama of nursery rhymes.

I connected the "very very good" side of the girl in the picture with her sweet, docile smile and pleasing nature and the "horrid" side of her with the straying curl.

The message was powerful. Personify the good side of the little girl: smile sweetly, be pleasing, do what's expected—no straying outside the lines. Suppress the mind-of-your-own dimension, which tends to sour everyone. In other words, when it comes to life, keep every hair in place.

It didn't take me long to learn the "good" set of expectations for little girls growing up in the fifties. Be pleasing, demure, compliant, conforming, docile, and sweet. Obtain what you need or want through charm, not directness. Be poised on the outside regardless of the chaos on the inside. Above all, smile.

As I experienced the frowns and internal bruises that came from occasional deviation from these expectations, my ego learned the Little Girl with a Curl way of being in the world. I learned how to please, how to adapt myself to the expectations of others and live out their projections of what a "good" girl should do and be. I spent a lot of time opening my parasol against the onslaughts of disapproval and put on my sweetest smile even when I didn't feel like smiling. I bent and spindled my soul trying to become what I perceived others wanted or needed from me.

The Little Girl with a Curl followed me right into adulthood. One day, over lunch, a prominent writer whom I admired expressed disdain for a social cause I supported. "I can't imagine how anyone could support such a cause," she said. "Can you?" I swallowed. My Girl with a Curl wanted very much to please her and have her approval. "No," I said weakly, "I suppose not." Later I felt sickened at how I'd compromised myself.

The Little Girl with a Curl is the part of us that says what we imagine people want to hear. She is, above all, a pleaser. In search of approval, she looks to others for her own validation.

When we give ourselves completely over to the idea and images of parents, husband, wife, church, social organizations, friends, or "prominent" persons, and silence our own voice of soul in the process, we allow others to create our sense of who we are rather than growing our own identity within ourselves. "Tell me what you want me to be and I'll be it."

It's amazing how many women remain stuck at this girlish level of development. It's understandable, though, when you realize how much around us encourages it. Everybody loves a pleaser. People who exhibit a mind of their own, straying from the status quo, are less welcome. Look at the life of Jesus. He *wasn't* a pleaser. Rather than adapt to expectations, he lovingly dared to be his own person. You see where it got him.

The task of the Little Girl with a Curl is to "author-ize" herself, as Sam Keen puts it.[15] With God she becomes the co-author of her own life rather than allowing herself to be authored by others.

Tinsel Star

When my daughter was small she got the dubious part of the Bethlehem star in a Christmas play. After her first rehearsal she burst through the door with her costume, a five-pointed star lined in shiny gold tinsel designed to drape over her like a sandwich board. "What exactly will you be doing in the play?" I asked her.

"I just stand there and shine," she told me. I've never forgotten that response.

As I named my false selves, it occurred to me that her part in the play was like a scene from my own life. I'd spent some time standing around trying to shine.

The Tinsel Star pours herself into a long line of praiseworthy accomplishments. She's the overachiever in us, the perfectionist, the performer whose outer radiance often covers an inner insecurity. Whether it's being mom, career woman, PTA grade-mother, church volunteer, or committee chair, the Tinsel Star's aim is to do it with dazzle and win accolades.

When we adopt this particular ego mask, we invest ourselves in the notion that those who shine the brightest are loved the most. This comes from the distorted idea that meaning and acceptance come from what we do, not who we are. We buy into the widespread notion that "light" emanates from our achievements, not from the divine fire within our soul.

Many years ago I hosted an afternoon tea in my home for a group of women. Aware how elaborate their own teas had been, I fussed for days over lace napkins, flower arrangements, china, silver, gourmet bread and butter sculpted into flower shapes (no, I'm not kidding). One guest said, "You've really outdone yourself today." I think she meant it as a compliment, but her words nailed me to a sudden truth. I was *trying* to outdo, outshine everyone—even myself. I wasn't motivated by hospitality and friendship but by the Star's need to impress. When it was over, I went outside and sat in the garden, asking God's forgiveness and trying to come to terms with my need to shine.

Accomplishments and achievements are well and good, but they need to flow out of a healthy motivation. Otherwise, when they cease we experience an empty darkness. The Star's task is to discover her own inner light, the divine spark, so that she doesn't constantly struggle to create light and warmth for herself by giving a lustrous performance.

Rapunzel

The story of Rapunzel, recounted in *Grimm's Fairy Tales*, reveals a false-self pattern common to many of us at certain times in our life. Rapunzel was a damsel imprisoned by a witch in a tower without a door. The only access to the tower was through a solitary window at the top. When the witch wanted to visit, she stood below and called for Rapunzel to let down her long, golden hair from the window. Then the witch scampered up, using Rapunzel's hair as a ladder. Year after year Rapunzel sat in the tower, singing sad songs and waiting for someone to come along and rescue her.

As I identified my false selves, I recognized Rapunzel in myself. She was the part of me that wanted Daddy, Mama, husband, or somebody else to come fix it, the part that languished in whatever struggle I found myself, singing sad songs and looking outside instead of inside for help.

Rapunzel is the helpless damsel waiting for rescue. Locked in a "towering" problem or difficulty, she waits for deliverance rather than taking responsibility for herself. Her waiting is *negative* waiting, not the creative, active waiting that initiates growth.

As I thought of Rapunzel, stuck all those years in a tower without a door, I wondered why Rapunzel couldn't figure out a way to get out. After all, the witch had been ingenious enough to figure out

how to get her in there in the first place. When I reread the tale—
especially the ending, where the witch, in a fury, picks up a pair of
shears and cuts off Rapunzel's hair—I wondered why it had never
dawned on Rapunzel to cut off her hair herself and use it as a
ladder. The answer was there all along, only she was so busy
waiting for rescue that she didn't see it.

It's important to be able to ask for and accept help, but not
Rapunzel's way. She chose to forego the contemplative experience
of tapping her soul-strength, to bury her problem-solving potential
and project it onto others. Struggling with the difficulties of life, we
may adopt the idea that we're too weak, too dumb, too busy, or too
incompetent to take care of ourselves and extricate ourselves from
pain and problems. A tape recording plays in our heads: You can't
manage that. You aren't able to figure it out yourself. You're too
weak to do it on your own.

When that happens, Rapunzel makes her grand appearance.

The Rapunzel pattern reminds me of an insight that pastoral
counselor and Episcopal priest Jean Clift received while watching
the opening credits of the television program "Mystery" on PBS. As
the credits roll, a cartoon-animated woman whose ankles are tied
waves her hands in the air and cries, "Ohhh! Ohhh!" waiting for
someone to come untie her.

"I watched that show for a long while before it occurred to me
that the woman's hands aren't tied," Jean said. "She could, if she
were so inclined, bend down and untie her own ankles."

That perceived helplessness is the sort of thing Rapunzel feels.

In the midst of my midlife pain, I wrote in my journal about a
similar fairy tale motif: "Sometimes I feel like Sleeping Beauty,
waiting for the kiss that never comes." Later I read that entry and
saw that I mustn't depend solely on others to bring the "kiss" to
heal me. I had to do it myself, with God's grace and Presence. I
needed to embrace myself, knowing that sometimes God's arms
were my arms. I needed to seek help, yes; but I also needed to bend
down and untie my own ankles. That's Rapunzel's task.

The Bible reminds us that "God did not give us a spirit of timidity but a spirit of power and love..." (2 Tim. 1:7). Or, as Paul wrote, "When I am weak, then I am strong" (2 Cor. 12:10). We have a formidable Spirit within us that makes us strong even when our ankles are tied.

Little Red Hen

I heard a storyteller say that people sometimes grow up and live out their favorite childhood stories. That caused me to wince. One of my favorites was the tale of the Little Red Hen.

This hen "did it all." She cooked, washed, made beds, swept, mended, hoed, raked, and mowed. She was a virtual whiz hen. One day she found some grains of wheat and asked her household companions who would help her plant them. "Not I," said the cat. "Not I," said the dog. "Not I," said the mouse. "Then I'll do it myself," said the Little Red Hen. And she did.

That becomes the litany of the story. Each time the hen asked for help—when she asked who would help her cut the wheat, grind it into flour, and make a cake—she received the same answer. So, with efficiency and resignation, she did it herself. In many ways the Little Red Hen is the opposite of Rapunzel; she's fully competent, with a self-sufficient exterior. Inside, however, she's gritting her teeth.

The pattern of the Little Red Hen is that of a martyr. Long-suffering and driven, she never stops. She's ruled by a duty-at-all-costs mentality and gives unceasingly—to the point of her own spiritual bankruptcy and mental exhaustion. Feeling the need to meet everyone's demands, she abdicates herself and becomes the victim.

The Little Red Hen rarely comes out to play. Life for her is a relentless chore, with few moments of spontaneity and exuberance. She's frozen her playfulness; no longer is she that delighting and delightful inner child who knows that sometimes a graceful wasting of time invites a holy encounter and puts one in touch with the true Center, the place where, as Eckhart observed, God and the soul are "eternally at play."

The martyr structure in my life was most evident in my role as the dutiful wife, sacrificing mother, and ambitious career woman. Even when the well inside was dust-dry, I usually kept on working and giving—sometimes through clenched teeth. In years past I had resisted the need to get away for a couple of days (or even hours) to replenish myself and listen to the unique music deep in my soul. I said such things as, "Go off on a retreat alone? But who would care for my family? Who would cook for them? They would surely starve. And what about the project I'm working on? I can't leave it now!" In other words, "I'll do it myself."

A woman caught in the martyr pattern once told me, "We're raised to be givers, even when it mutilates us. When it comes to giving to myself, my name isn't on the gift list. If it ever turned up, it would be dead last."

The Little Red Hen would have us believe that we should do our duty with silent contentment at the expense of ourselves. One of my favorite Gary Larson cartoons shows two cows in a pasture. One is saying to the other, "I don't care what they say. I'm not content." Dis-contentment comes when we sense a loss of our inner content. It isn't a bad thing when it causes us to look within and seek our soul, however. That's *holy* discontent.

In the story the Little Red Hen reached that state eventually. After planting the grains, harvesting them, grinding the flour, and baking the cake—all herself—the hen asked, "Now who will help me eat the cake?" Naturally everybody showed up. Suddenly something snapped in the Little Red Hen. "No, you won't!" she shouted. "I'll eat it myself!"

Inside every Little Red Hen something is seething. A friend of mine who's an outwardly "contented" woman with a husband, three children, and a creative gift as an artist told me, "I get up at 6:00 A.M. and don't stop all day just so that everything will go smoothly for my husband and children. Their needs are met to perfection, but hardly any of my own needs are met. I never have time for myself—to feed the creative spark in me. I give up everything, suppress everything inside me, for others."

As she spoke I could feel the resentment rising in her veins; I noticed her fists tightening. "I need to do something about it, but I have voices in and around me that insist that the most important thing in life isn't creativity or joy or even wholeness; the most important thing is *duty!*" Suddenly one fist came crashing down on the table. "I think one day I'm going to explode!"

I think you just have, I said to myself. Indeed, her hardened martyr structure was showing a few cracks. She was finally facing her own holy discontent. That encounter reminded me of something I read in a beautiful little book called *Knowing Woman*: "Duty and love are miles apart."[16]

While speaking at a women's retreat, I mentioned the story of my artist friend. A participant came up to me afterward and said, "But putting others first and oneself last is a woman's calling in life. We're supposed to always give and be servants no matter what, and I wish you wouldn't tell me differently!" As she spoke, she raised her hands to cover her ears. It can be threatening to hear something that rubs against the grooves of the should's and ought's carved into our lives.

I believe that a healthy sharing of oneself is a holy call, but so is caring for ourselves and taking time for the beautiful mysteries God created within us. The important thing is balance. Being a martyr distorts the virtuous ideal of giving to others by crossing over into victim postures and a self-denial that squelches selfhood and the creative life of the soul.

The Bible summons us to self-love as well as other-love: "Love your neighbor *as yourself*" (Matt. 22:39). How are we ever going to truly love others if we don't cultivate self-love? (Not narcissistic love, but healthy self-accepting love.) The person who doesn't love herself is usually the one who's most preoccupied with herself, who's most selfish.

The task of the Little Red Hen is twofold. First, she must learn to love herself extravagantly, which is the way God loves her. In order to free ourselves from the martyr mask we need to learn how to treat ourselves compassionately, to balance our giving. When I was wrapped up in my driven martyrdom, a teasing friend once told me, "If you treated others the way you treat yourself, you'd get arrested."

Second, the Little Red Hen must learn how to come out and play. She needs to turn loose her grown-up stoicism and rigid control and say yes not only to herself but to life.

One day my friend Betty and I took a walk together. As we strolled along, we muttered about the demands and pressures of work and about how compulsive we sometimes become trying to do it all.

Suddenly we came upon a deserted playground. Our pace slowed, then stopped. We sat shyly in the swings and dangled our feet. I could sense the child in each of us trying to come out—the giggling little girl who used to swing so high that the soles of her tennis shoes seemed to skim the clouds.

We tossed each other a why-not shrug and shoved off. As we swang higher and higher, we laughed and sang, freeing something lost and precious inside. Time melted away; the moments disappeared into sacred bliss.

Today Betty and I recall that occasion with wonder, knowing that it reunited us with that part of ourselves that's eternally at play with God and life. It helped heal the Little Red Hen in each of us.

Tin Woodman

One of the more destructive patterns we can take on is that of a person cut off from her feelings, from her heart. That pattern isn't uncommon, as Djohariah Toor notes:

Many women are wounded at the heart level because our culture has generally diverted itself from feeling. We can be emotional, but this doesn't mean we can recognize and articulate feelings. The fact is, a lot of women are *afraid* to feel. . . . Emotionally we are immobilized, bound to convention and a masculine penchant to keep a stiff upper lip.[17]

Many of us learned to be afraid of the feelings inside ourselves. Perhaps when we risked expressing them, we met with astonishment and admonishment, which led to embarrassment and vulnerability. So gradually we built an ego structure in which we separated ourselves from our feelings and avoided deep self-disclosure, even to ourselves.

While reading Frank L. Baum's *Wizard of Oz* with my daughter, I identified this pattern as the Tin Woodman—a character in the book who had no heart. He represents the part of us that's cut off from our feelings.

In the story Dorothy found the Tin Woodman, completely rusted over, standing with his axe uplifted. She ran for an oil can and gave him a good squirt. Released at last, the Tin Woodman told Dorothy that he had once been a real person with a real body, in love with a young woman he planned to marry. The Witch of the East had enchanted his axe, however, causing him to cut off both legs. He replaced these with tin. Then he cut off his arms and again replaced them with tin. Finally his entire body had been cut away and replaced with tin. He was no longer covered in warm flesh but was trapped in an unfeeling armor.

This can be a familiar story in our lives. Whenever we come under the sway of those inner forces that censure and fragment us, we become progressively disconnected from how we really feel, from the passionate voice of our heart. We rust over. There comes a time in life when, like Dorothy, we need to run for the oil can.

Reading through my journal I came upon words that read like the voice of the Tin Woodman, like the voice of a woman searching for her heart:

I ask myself, When I glimpse a hummingbird in my tulips, can I call up my gladness and spend some time with it? And a stern voice in me says,

How wasteful—what if you don't get everything done? I ask, Can I allow myself to feel the pain of a relationship that needs rekindling? No, the voice says. Stifle it and pretend. Rocked boats tip over. So I ask, What about the anger inside? Can I feel it? And the voice says, It's not nice to be angry. Then I ask, When I'm scared and hurting, can I open my soul and let someone peer way down inside? And it says, Keep a stiff upper lip. Bury it.

When I live with those answers long enough, I can no longer connect to my real feelings. I lose my ability to relate to myself and others from a genuine place. I lose myself.

Such a split of the head from the heart is common in our culture. Along with this goes another painful splitting: the severing of our body from our soul. As we separate from our feelings, we tend to separate from our bodies as well. Gradually they are cut away. When this happens, we become alienated from our earthiness, our sexuality, and the connecting relation that knits our soul to our body in a wholesome way.

In this separation we see our sexuality in a narrow way. Yet sex isn't merely an act; it's a wide and natural range of energies, instincts, and responses to life. It's a vast, creative current of life energy that flows inside us.

Unfortunately, a lot of us learned to fear and mistrust sexuality. Growing up, I tended to polarize my sexuality and my instincts from the rest of me. I knew they were there, but I wasn't terribly connected to them.

In the Church especially we're inclined to incorporate a view of matter as sinful and the body as a fallen creation. In the Bible the word *flesh* is used negatively, to be sure. But we've misread things by connecting that word to our sexuality. The word, as used in the Bible, doesn't refer to skin and bones and the beautiful weavings of the human body. John Westerhoff tells us that it refers to the power of sin and death, which encompasses both body and soul. He says that to live in flesh is to live a life that *denies* our bodies.[18]

I meet lots of women who've been wounded in this area. Because of this woundedness, a lot of us have split off our bodies, our sensual, sexual side and pushed them away. We've made these parts of us orphans. We can do that in a number of ways, according to Djohariah Toor: by acting promiscuously, by fleeing into our spiritual and intellectual lives, or by cutting off our instincts altogether.[19]

At times I tended to ignore my feeling, sexual side by living in the airy spaces of spirit and intellect. Believing that the workings of my mind were superior to my feelings, and that my spirit was much more important than my body, I tended to live in my head. Yet God didn't prioritize the parts of me. God created my emotions, my instincts, my senses, and my body as well as my spirit and my mind—and pronounced them all "good."

I was more able to accept the value of my physical self when I realized that incarnation occurred in connection with the body, that Mary birthed Christ through her *flesh*, portraying a marriage of matter and spirit. It was a dazzling idea to me, a healing idea.

In increasing ways I began to learn that we birth the True Self, the Christ-life, in communion with the *whole* of ourselves. Eckhart proclaimed, "The soul loves the body,"[20] and Hildegard sang of the joy that comes from bringing the two together in mutual reverence. Yet many of us negate this part of ourselves—the heart-in-the-body part, that dancing, feeling, sexual, sensual part. Part of our healing involves rediscovering the great life-energy we've locked up. Then we can learn to adopt this part of us back and relate to it in healthy, God-given ways.

I recognized that my waiting would involve calling up this repressed part of me and healing my separation. It would mean learning to live my journey in a circle of oneness—in thought *and* emotion, soul *and* body, spirituality *and* sexuality. I sensed that a part of being whole in the spiritual life meant acknowledging the feelings trickling, pouring, and sometimes raging through my heart, as well as integrating the music and instincts of my body.

I'm discovering that a spiritual journey is a lot like a poem. You don't merely recite a poem or analyze it intellectually. You dance it, sing it, cry it, feel it on your skin and in your bones. You move with it and feel its caress. It falls on you like a teardrop or wraps around you like a smile. It lives in the heart and the body as well as the spirit and the head.

The task of the Tin Woodman is to welcome back her feelings, embrace her body, and discover God in *all* of herself.

Chicken Little

Another way some of us cope with the slings and arrows that threaten our fragile egos is to construct a Chicken Little defense. Chicken Little, you'll remember, was ambling along when an acorn fell on her head. Her fear exaggerated the acorn into a piece of the sky and she scurried into a cave crying, "The sky is falling! The sky is falling!"

This is the pattern of retreating from life and protecting ourselves from rejection and uncertainty by finding a cave of safety in which to hide. When we wear the Chicken Little mask, we believe the sky is always about to fall. Albert Einstein said that the most important question was whether the universe is friendly. Chicken Little has answered that with an unequivocal no. She withdraws in fear and avoids situations that present risk—inner or outer. Obviously there are times when it's best not to risk. But she's the part of us that dares too little, especially on the inside.

Chicken Little, like all the other false selves, has been wounded on some level and has created her pattern as a way of coping with her pain and protecting herself. Perhaps she was overprotected; perhaps she had experiences that taught her that life couldn't be trusted. Chicken Little, with her egocentric pattern, is similar to what Fritz Kunkel called the "Turtle."[21] This is the person who, believing that her needs are being neglected and that life doles out disappointments, restricts herself and pulls into a shell from which she peeps out at life.

We all have a touch of Chicken Little at times. Growing up, I thought I wanted to be a nurse. When I made this decision public, I began to get biographies of Florence Nightingale and little nurse kits for my birthday. If someone cut a finger, I got called in as the designated bandager. I became a candystriper at the hospital, earned my B.S. degree in nursing, and worked in the field for many years before I acknowledged that deep inside of me was a writer, not a nurse.

Immediately I became Chicken Little. I thought that if I gave up my safe, prescribed role as a nurse and risked being a writer, the sky would fall. I went around muttering, "What if I make a fool of myself? What if I fail? What will my family think if I leave a perfectly good career? And for what? To be a writer, for pete's sake. How absurd!" It was just another way of chanting, "The sky is falling! The sky is falling!"

Now and then, in the search for your True Self, you have to find the courage to enter a great absurdity. Kierkegaard pointed out that courage isn't the absence of despair and fear but the capacity to move ahead in spite of them.[22] The task of Chicken Little is to move ahead in spite of her fear by affirming the world as a loving, beautiful, safe place and God as her beloved companion in it. She must claim the mystical knowledge of Julian of Norwich, who said that (no matter what) "all shall be well and all manner of things shall be well." Chicken Little needs to trust that the sky isn't all that precarious and let an acorn be an acorn.

There's a verse in the Bible especially for Chicken Littles: "He commanded the skies above, and...he rained down upon them manna to eat" (Ps. 78:23–24). What we need to envision falling on us from the sky is God's nourishment, that's all. This means leaning out into the unknown spaces of faith and risk.

THE EMBRACING

There are some memorable lines in Arthur Miller's *After the Fall* that speak to the dilemma of the false selves:

> I had the same dream each night—that I had a child, and even in the dream I saw that the child was my life; and it was an idiot, and I ran away. Until I thought, if I could kiss it...perhaps I could rest. And I bent to its broken face, and it was horrible...but I kissed it. I think one must finally take one's life in one's arms.[23]

In naming the many patterns of our false selves, that's exactly what we need to do: bend down to the broken, horrible faces in ourselves and kiss each one.

That's the necessary act. For in such tender but powerful acts of self-communion, we make a way for the true seed to break through the folds of darkness. Only by confronting the false selves and embracing them can we liberate the True Self.

That spring I received a card from a friend. She had stuck a slip of paper inside with a quote on it by Mary Howitt: "He is happiest who hath power to gather wisdom from a flower." I immediately thought back to the daffodil bulbs in my garden, to the wisdom God had offered me through their yellow petals. And yes, it did give me cause to be happy.

PASSAGE OF
SEPARATION

CHAPTER 4

Crisis as Opportunity

Dorothy stood in the doorway with Toto in her arms, and looked at the sky....Suddenly Uncle Henry stood up. "There's a cyclone coming, Em," he called....There came a great shriek from the wind, and the house shook so hard Dorothy lost her footing....The great pressure of the wind on every side of the house raised it up higher and higher, until it was at the very top of the cyclone; and there it remained and was carried miles and miles away.

FRANK L. BAUM

The only way the Self can manifest is through conflict.

MARIE-LOUISE VON FRANZ

On the eve of the spring equinox the sky turned charcoal gray and the trees in the backyard began to bend and swirl. I went to the back door to call the dogs inside before the rain started. A lawn chair had blown off the patio, along with two flower pots which the wind was tossing through the grass. Spring wasn't going to come gently.

I gazed at the brewing surface of the sky, at the dark wind and serrated clouds, and for one penetrating moment I was aware that what I was seeing—the stormy contents of my backyard—was something happening on the inside of me too, on a terrain just as real.

I looked at the crab-apple tree. My cocoon swung precariously on the limb where I'd taped it. I ran to the tree, dodging the first

77

pellets of rain. Unwinding the tape, I carried the little cocoon inside, the dogs barking and trailing after me.

For lack of a better place, I stuck the twig on which the cocoon was attached in a pot of African violets on my desk, then toweled myself and the dogs dry. I returned to my writing, but I couldn't concentrate. I found myself staring at the chrysalis, at this lump of brown silence. It overwhelmed me with its simple truth. *A creature can separate from an old way of existence, enter a time of metamorphosis, and emerge to a new level of being.*

THE THREEFOLD CYCLE OF WAITING

In that moment it struck me clearly that the waiting process actually has three distinct phases that need to be maneuvered: *separation, transformation, and emergence.* Looking into the heart of that little cocoon, I knew that I had come upon the inner maze of waiting.

The life of the soul evolves and grows as we move through these three cycles. The process isn't a one-time experience but a spiraling journey that we undertake throughout life. Life is full of cocoons. We die and are reborn again and again. By repeatedly entering the spiral of separation, transformation, and emergence, we're brought closer each time to wholeness and the True Self.

I picked up my Bible and turned the pages, becoming aware of how God had revealed this ageless process in its stories. I pored over the Old Testament story of the Hebrew's exodus from Egypt. I read it not only as a chronicle of salvation history but as the story of an inner journey taking place within the landscape of one's soul.

Egypt, wilderness, and *promised land* are comparable to interior states of being: *larva, cocoon,* and *butterfly.* In both journeys—inward and outward—there's first a movement of separation, then a holding environment where transformation happens, and finally an emergence into a new existence.

The Israelite slave represents a person in a larval stage of inner development. She lives an existence in which authentic parts of herself are imprisoned. The True Self isn't yet liberated. Enslaved by the false selves of the ego, she believes that Egypt is all there is. Day after day she makes bricks out of straw, oblivious to the horizons in her own soul.

At a "burning bush" moment the divine fire inside is struck and the summons to separation or exodus comes. It precipitates a crisis, an uprising within. Plagues and doubts ensue. Shall I leave Egypt or not? How can I extricate myself? What awaits me if I go? The "pharaoh" inside her, which represents the powerful voice of the status quo, does everything possible to keep her enslaved. The decision to allow the uprising and see it through despite the risks propels her out of Egypt. She undergoes a stormy Red Sea crossing, a final letting go of the old way, and enters the second phase of the process: the cocoon of the wilderness.

The wilderness symbolizes the inner place where she's stripped to her essence, forced to wander the abyss of her own depths. She waits without answers, trusting God for the nourishment she can't produce herself, making covenants with the unseen new.

When that step is completed, she enters the third phase of the process, emerging into the promised land, into a new way of being and relating. Something new and holy within her is set free. She begins to live from the promised place God has created within her.

THE NIGHT SEA JOURNEY

I lowered my Bible. Outside, the wind howled. I leaned back in my chair, filled with the beauty of the interior exodus, trying to think of other biblical examples that express the same inner passages of separation, transformation, and emergence.

Maybe it was the rain splashing against the house that inspired me, because the next thing I knew I was reading the story of Jonah.

It opened up to me as a vivid metaphoric journey of waiting and transformation. I read it through tears, for it was *my* story.

A voice interrupted Jonah's secure world—a holy summons to go to Ninevah, the new place. It reminded me of the voice of change and crisis that had sliced open my own safe world and beckoned me to newness.

Like a lot of us, Jonah resisted separation from his old way of life. Hopping a ship, he tried to run away. A storm then arose, and God is depicted as hurling the winds. In the same way, crisis winds often grow more turbulent as we resist the voice of the soul. Our difficulties become, as we say, a "full-blown" crisis.

As the storm worsened, Jonah hid in the bottom of the ship. Finally, fearing that everyone would perish, he surrendered to the experience. He came out of hiding and let go, offering himself to be cast into the sea. This is the moment of descent into one's inner depths. In this act Jonah completed the separation and entered the phase of transformation.

As he was swallowed into the belly of a great fish, Jonah entered the cocoon—the dark womb in the sea where his metamorphosis took place. Here we allow ourselves to be "digested"—to be changed in substance. (No wonder we've made this story into a Bible tale for children. It's much too scary for us adults.)

Years ago I told the story of Jonah to my six-year-old vacation Bible school class, and the children fell into a discussion about how they would manage to escape if swallowed like Jonah. "I'd start a fire in the whale's stomach and he'd cough me out!" declared one fellow, no doubt remembering the scene from Pinocchio.

"I'd stomp on his tongue till he spit me out," said another. The suggestions grew wilder by the minute. Suddenly a thoughtful little girl spoke up: "I'd call my daddy and wait till he got me out." All these years later her simple wisdom still resonated in me: call on God and wait.

That's exactly what Jonah did. But he didn't wait in helpless passivity as Rapunzel did in the tower. He waited *actively*—letting go, descending into the depths of his soul, listening, opening himself to change, praying. His cry from the whale's belly formed the hue and texture of my own midlife prayer: "I called to the Lord, out of my distress, and he answered me; . . . out of the belly of Sheol I cried, and thou didst hear my voice. For thou didst cast me into the deep, into the heart of the seas. . . . The waters closed in over me, the deep was round about me" (Jon. 2:2–3, 5).

Waiting is allowing holy waters to close over you. It means having the deep round about you. It means taking the "night sea journey."

In Joseph Campbell's book *The Hero with a Thousand Faces* there's a picture of the "Night Sea Journey" portrayed in three panels. The first panel shows Joseph being lowered into the well by his brothers. The second shows Christ being placed in the tomb. The third shows Jonah being swallowed by a whale. Campbell wrote that the imagery in each panel suggests that a person "goes inward, to be born again."[1] We don't cross into the "sphere of rebirth" by power but by descent, by being swallowed.

The last phase, emergence, begins after Jonah's symbolic three days and nights are completed and he's released from the fish. He emerges as a new person on the shoreline of Ninevah. He has come upon the new horizon inside himself.

I closed the Bible, the imagery of the night sea journey alive in me. I saw myself in the midst of my own midlife tempest. I glanced toward the window. It was just as I'd imagined when I watched the storm lifting the contents of the backyard—the event really *was* happening inside me. Like Jonah, I had been lifted into the windy spaces of my own soul.

I let out a long, slow breath. For the first time since it all began, I felt myself relax into the storm. I wasn't so afraid of it now. God's presence was round about me.

That moment spoke a great truth to me. We can endure, transcend, and transform the storminess when we see the meaning and mystery of it.

SOURCES OF CRISIS

When my son was ten, he spent an entire afternoon in the carport arranging hundreds of dominoes. He planned to set off a chain reaction so that they would fall in perfect sequence, the last one falling from the top of a little ramp into a bucket of water. He wanted to end with a splash, he explained.

With the last domino in place, he came inside to summon me to the big event. When we got to the carport, we found a dog lumbering through his creation. The whole thing was wrecked. My first thought was to chase the dog with a broom, at the very least, yell at it. Bob's response was different, however. He sighed deeply, then went over and gave the dog a pat on the head. As he regrouped the dominoes, I asked him, "Didn't that upset you?"

"Yes, but stuff like this happens, Mama," he told me.

So it does. I don't hold to the idea that God *causes* suffering and crisis. I just know that those things come along and God uses them. We think life should be a nice, clean ascending line. But inevitably something wanders onto the scene and creates havoc with the nice way we've arranged life to fall in place. As my son taught me, those disruptions are part of life too. Stuff happens. You might as well pat the dog and regroup.

It helps if we understand the source of the crisis. There are three basic sources: developmental transitions, intrusive events, and internal uprisings.

Developmental Transitions

The natural developmental transitions through which we move from one season of life to another are as unavoidable as the dog that wandered through Bob's dominoes.

As I struggled to make sense of my life, I wondered if what I was experiencing as a crisis was typical. Did others face what I felt? As I delved into some truths from developmental psychology, my experience grew more understandable.

I discovered that developmental transitions are like the tapered neck of an hourglass—difficult but necessary passages that we have to navigate in order to emerge into the next era of life. In Daniel Levinson's celebrated study of life's stages I found four natural developmental transitions delineated: early childhood, to age three; early adulthood, from seventeen to twenty-two; midlife, from forty to forty-five; and late adulthood from sixty to sixty-five.[2] Levinson points out that these transitions are also times of termination; we must accept the losses each transition brings. The transitions are seeded with imbalance and turmoil, and how we cross each of them has an inevitable and decided impact on the era of life that follows.

I remembered, too, that back in college I'd studied Erik Erikson's famous eight stages of life-development as "crisis" periods.[3] His idea was that in each stage of life we're presented with two conflicting possibilities, and we need to resolve each conflict successfully in order to emerge maturely into the next era of life.

What did he have to say about midlife? That period coincides with the crisis Erikson called "generativity vs. stagnation." On one side, the person experiences a tug toward growth, a need to draw on deeper internal resources to create a revitalized participation in life. On the other side, she feels the pull to stagnate, to become "static, stuck,...bogged down in a life full of obligation and devoid of self-fulfillment."[4]

I received a letter from a sixty-two-year old reader who had read an article I'd written on growing older. She told me about a developmental crisis in her life that arose from a natural developmental transition. She wrote as follows:

I was finishing a nice meal when the waitress brought the check. She informed me that the restaurant had given me their senior citizen discount. Well, I can't really describe it, but all at once I felt jolted. I'm becoming an old woman, I thought. A cloud fell over me. Ever since, I've been facing things, trying to come to terms with what's ahead. I know it will be different, but I'm determined it won't be diminishing.

She glimpsed the import of the "cloud" that fell over her and decided to confront the task of her transition, which according to Erikson is to find meaning and value while coming to terms with death. How she deals with it will make all the difference in her experience of the last epoch of life.

Intrusive Events

The second source of crisis comes from intrusive events that impinge on us from without. These crises come in many forms and usually take us by surprise. A death, an illness, an accident, a lost job, a broken relationship, an unwelcome move, a dashed dream, an empty nest, a betrayal.

It may be unwise (probably even insensitive) to suggest to someone at this point that the calamity can be a transformative event. There's a fullness of time for such an awareness, a fluidity to the crisis that must be allowed. When the awareness does manage to break through, however, it can assume the impact of Abraham Maslow's "peak event" or William James's "epiphany."

My friend Betty had an intrusive crisis event several years ago. In her early forties she was diagnosed with lung and breast cancer and given a rotten prognosis for recovery. I sat with her one day while she cried wrenching tears, feeling that my heart was going to explode along with hers. I couldn't say to her, "Yes, but just you wait; this could be a transforming crisis." At the outset, what mattered was survival. "I will not die!" she cried. "I will not! Do you hear me?"

"I hear you," I told her. But we both knew it was some deep part of herself that she most wanted to hear those words.

She lived her crisis with raw honesty. As the weeks passed, I watched her pound a pillow with her fist in outraged indignation that such a thing could happen to her. I watched her sink. I watched her hold herself with utter love and whisper bleeding prayers.

Then one day it seemed to me she was different. "What's happened?" I asked her. She smiled, and if I live to be 110 I'll never forget the beauty in her soul at that moment. She told me, "I looked death in the eyes and I said, 'I want to live! But if I die, I die. And it will be well.' I can't explain it, Sue, but in that moment something in my innermost being shifted. I knew that my experience with cancer was going to be the most transforming journey of my life. Whatever happens, I'm going to be okay."

She had come upon the "epiphany" buried in her crisis—the creative moment that can't be forced, only discovered and chosen. Her crisis was the transforming crucible of her life. It propelled her into a new and deeper journey that she continues to this day.

Internal Uprisings

A third source of crisis, internal uprisings, is less easy to identify. Such uprisings are the myriad of agonies that flare up within us.

An internal uprising could be as simple as a vague sense of restlessness, some floating disenchantment, a whispering but relentless voice that says, There *has* to be more than this. Why are you doing what you're doing?

Or the uprising may take the form of stress, burnout, a chronic sense of exhaustion, inner voices desperately trying to tell us something. Perhaps an addiction grows too loud to ignore any longer, or the scar tissue of an old wound begins to break down and we have to face the place where life has impaled us.

A common uprising involves an eruption of fear and doubt concerning God and faith. That was the case of a woman who approached me at a conference in southern California. She introduced herself as "a minister's wife" and asked if she could speak with me.

"For months I've been fighting a terrible realization," she confided. "I can no longer believe in the God I was brought up with. That God has vanished. I keep trying to go back to the way it was before. But I only end up pretending. I feel smothered by the lie I'm living, but I'm terrified of what will happen if I face the doubts inside."

She was standing on the rim of a crisis that believers may actually need in order to keep growing. In his book *Soul Making*, Alan Jones writes of the questions of faith that act as agents inviting us to a deeper spiritual experience.[5] He has found that they correspond to the experiences of the apostles.

The first spins around the question, What will I do with my life? This was the question the apostles faced when they decided to leave their fishing boats. It leads us into an initial conversion, with which we're all familiar. We follow Christ and life is made new. Our conversion is glorious, as it was for the apostles when they left their nets. (Christ was healing and teaching, the crowds were coming, and the apostles were at the hub of it.) When things go wrong, it's to that conversion that we inevitably try to return. We want to make it happen again.

The next question of faith comes when things in our lives begin to fall apart. Something wrecks the dominoes. For the apostles, it was Jesus' crucifixion. The life that they had known with him was taken away. They felt numb, betrayed; it was as if the God they had invested everything in had vanished. They could no longer believe as they had before. Jones says that it's as if their egoism were being burned out. Now the disciples have to go deeper and find a faith that allows them to live not only with the presense of Christ but with his seeming absence. They have to enter the darkness of their own doubts and come through to a faith that is true to where they are *now*.

It seemed to me that the woman at the conference was experiencing this latter struggle. Identifying her crisis in this new light became her creative moment. She was able to journey on to a deeper and more honest faith.

Throughout life we experience crises from many sources: from natural developmental transitions, from events that intrude from without, and from conditions that rise up within. While it helps to understand the roots of our crises, we also need to recognize that no matter the source, they all have one thing in common—a threshold.

CRISIS AS SEPARATION AND OPPORTUNITY

A crisis is a holy summons to cross a threshold. It involves both a leaving behind and a stepping toward, a separation and an opportunity.

The word *crisis* derives from the Greek words *krisis* and *krino*, which mean "a separating." The very root of the word implies that our crises are times of severing from old ways and states of being. We need to ask ourselves what it is we're being asked to separate from. What needs to be left behind?

As I asked myself the question, I drew courage from a Bible story. One man who came to Jesus wanting to be a disciple said, "Let me first go and bury my father." Jesus gave him what seems like a harsh answer: "Follow me, and leave the dead to bury their own dead" (Matt. 8:21–22). But when you apply the answer to the process of inner transformation, it makes perfect sense. This is a call to separation. To "leave the dead." In order to follow the inner journey, we need to leave behind those things that are deadening, the loyalties that no longer have life for us.

Crisis is a separation, but it's equally a time of opportunity. The Chinese word for *crisis* is composed of two characters. On top is the sign for danger; beneath it is the sign for opportunity. That character graphically illustrates the saying, "Crisis is really another name for redirection."

A minister friend of mine, who has seen countless Christians through crisis events, told me that he didn't think most Christians knew *how* to have a crisis—at least not creatively.

He started me wondering. For the most part, we do one of two things in response to a crisis. We say that it's God's will and force ourselves into an outwardly sweet acceptance, remaining unaffected at the deeper level of the spirit. People who have a crisis in this manner are generally after comfort and peace of mind.

Or we reject the crisis, fighting and railing against it until we become cynical and defeated or suffer a loss of faith. People who choose this way to have a crisis are after justice.

Yet there's a third way to have a crisis: the way of waiting. That way means creating a painfully honest and contemplative relationship with one's own depths, with God in the deep center of one's soul. People who choose this way aren't so much after peace of mind or justice as wholeness and transformation. They're after soulmaking.

If you choose this way, you find the threshold, the creative moment or epiphany, within the crisis. You discover that the stormy experience can be an agent drawing you deeper into the kingdom, separating you from the old consciousness and the clamp of the ego. It's not an easy way. As John Sanford notes,

At first the approach of the kingdom may seem like a violent attack from something dark and dreadful. . . . Entrance into the kingdom means the destruction of the old personality with its constricted and uncreative attitudes. . . . The fortress behind which the ego had been hiding must be torn down, and as these defenses are battered down forcibly by the movements from within, it may seem at first like a violent assault.[6]

It may seem that way, of course, but as theologian Martin Marty writes, "Brokenness and wounding do not occur in order to break human dignity but to open the heart so God can act."[7]

Jesus had some curious things to say about the way a person comes into the inner kingdom of the True Self. You do it, he said, by entering a "narrow gate," which only a few folks ever find (Luke 13:24). You do it by way of tight, difficult, uncomfortable places that separate you out from the rest of the herd.

In another biblical reference Jesus proclaimed, "I have come to bring fire to the earth" (Luke 12:49, JB). The coming of the inner kingdom often erupts through a fiery experience. That verse reminds me of the moment in the *Divine Comedy* when Dante enters the searing fire through which all persons must pass in order to make their way to Paradiso, the dwelling of God.

Dante is afraid of the flames; but he's assured that it's okay to enter, for this is the fire that burns but does not consume. To walk through this fire is not to die but to be transformed and purged. That is the fire of Christ.

FROM KANSAS TO OZ

While reading the *The Wizard of Oz*, I saw striking parallels between the inner quest for the True Self and Dorothy's journey from Kansas to Oz and back to Kansas. Essentially, her journey is the search for a way to come home.

The image of coming home is a powerful, archetypal symbol for returning to one's deepest self, to the soul. To come home is to return to the place of inner origin, that original imprint of God within. Therefore, coming home fills us with a sense of being in the right place, a sense of deep spiritual belonging. We all have this profound longing to come home, whether we recognize it or not.

Perhaps the root spiritual problem of our time is that modern people, even modern Christians, have lost their way home. Not only that, we've lost the directions to find it. There are few places within our scientific, rationalistic culture that have enough connection to the symbolic realm of soul to point the way. Even the Church seems at times to have forgotten its role as the custodian and guide of the way home. Rather than helping us grow our souls organically beneath our very own hearts and illuminating the way to the deep inner ground, it frequently majors in theological propositions, dogma, intellect, institutional agendas, and the shepherding of great flocks of should's and ought's. Jung once pointed out that religion can easily become a defense against an experience of God.

Without maps and signposts, people search for their inner home in the wrong places: in professional success, material status, institutions, persons, pleasure, and on and on. But none of these can ever be home. We end up spiritual refugees.

One day, while I was working in a homeless shelter in Atlanta, a homeless man said to me, "People have one of two reactions when they see me on the street. They either ignore me or despise me."

"Why do you think that is?" I asked him.

He turned his pained, watery eyes on me and said, "Because they see themselves, of course."

Of course. We see in this group of wandering souls the condition of our own spiritual homelessness, and we either despise them for showing it to us or we ignore them so that we don't have to be reminded of it.

Dorothy's is an inner journey of coming home to herself. Her longing for home is portrayed in her adventure through Oz so strongly that it almost seems to take on the life of another character.

The story begins in Kansas, which is described as a gray place. Not even the grass was green. The house in which Dorothy lived was as dull and gray as the prairie. It was also confining; the house had four walls and one room.

Living within the narrow confines of false selves, in one-room, four-walled roles, is like living in an interior Kansas. There life is reduced to narrow roles and expectations that leave little room for the deepest and truest part of ourselves to come out and breathe. The color always goes out of such a world.

My fascination grew as I read about the cyclone that tossed Dorothy's one-room existence into the air. When the tempest came, she was standing on the threshold of the too-small house. In that moment she received her call to go on the quest. It came through a crisis swooping down unexpectedly upon her. It was her moment of separation, her moment of opportunity.

The way the call came to Dorothy is frequently the way it comes to us. We lean on the threshold, unable to separate ourselves from ways of living that cramp the soul. It's usually at that precise moment that the cyclone appears. Some turbulence lifts our "house" into the air and turns our world upside down. With that, we're propelled into the journey.

The message that I discovered in Dorothy's cyclone was that crises can be holy beginnings if we allow them. If we listen, we'll hear God calling from the tumult, as God spoke to Job from a whirlwind.

When the cyclone struck, Aunt Em threw open a trap door in the floor and disappeared down a small, dark hole into the cellar, shouting for Dorothy to follow her. There's always the risk that we'll retreat into the security of the cellar rather than ride the cyclone to a new place.

While leading a women's retreat, I mentioned the "voice of Aunt Em" that seems to inhabit most of us. A woman who had gone through a crisis with an alcoholic son spoke up and said, "When my life fell around me, I picked up the pieces and put them back together the same way they were before. Nothing changed. When I did that, I was Aunt Em retreating into the small, dark hole in the cellar. I didn't ride the cyclone; I never left Kansas."

At the threshold moment, when the True Self within is demanding emergence, things can go either way. We can let the crisis thrust us into the heart of transformation or we can regress into our same old patterns.

Dorothy risked the whirlwind, and as a result she was carried miles from Kansas. The book describes her reaction:

> It was very dark, and the wind howled terribly around her. . . . Hour after hour passed away, and slowly Dorothy got over her fright. At first she had wondered if she would be dashed to pieces when the house fell again; but as the hours passed. . .she stopped worrying and resolved to *wait* calmly and see what the future would bring. [Italics added.][8]

Hope lies in braving the chaos and waiting calmly, with trust in the God who loves us. For if, like Dorothy, we wait, we may find that God delivers us somewhere amazing—into a place vibrant with color and startling encounters with the soul.

Dorothy arrived in a place that presented her with parts of herself: with a Scarecrow who had lost his brain and needed to learn to think for himself, a Tin Woodman who had lost his heart and needed to learn to feel his own feelings, and a Lion who had lost his courage and needed to find the inner mettle to be himself.

Walking such an inner spiral is the only way home. Dorothy walked the spiral and arrived back where she started, in Kansas. But Kansas wasn't the same. She came home to find a different house—one that was new and spacious.

Likewise, through our journey of waiting, we come home to live out a new, more expansive, more authentic vision of who we are. As T. S. Eliot wrote,

> We shall not cease from exploration
> And the end of all our exploring
> Will be to arrive where we started
> And know the place for the first time.[9]

PRAYER OF FAITH

To believe that you can find your way "home" through the crises and sufferings that fall upon you—and believe it even in the midnight of your struggle—requires a transfigured vision. It requires faith.

Teilhard de Chardin, Jesuit priest, paleontologist, and philosopher, asked for such faith when he prayed, "In all those dark moments, O God, grant that I may understand that it is you who are painfully parting the fibers of my being in order to penetrate to the very marrow of my substance. . . ."[10] That deep and beautiful prayer can help us learn to trust that inside us is a loving, divine power that heals and guides.

I find something breathtakingly hallowed about this truth: that in the midst of pain and crisis God is drawing us to wholeness. I prayed often for the faith to believe, to see that in my experience God was parting the fibers of my being. I struggled to trust that the whirlwind I was riding was a sacred opportunity—that it wanted to take me somewhere.

GROANINGS OF THE HEART

While a crisis is a summons into transformation, we must also recognize that it's an advent into an entanglement of feelings. Part of living a crisis creatively is identifying and understanding the feelings that come with it. Otherwise, we don't have a crisis; it has us.

As a little fellow my son used to walk around singing a line from a song that was popular at the time. It always came out, "Feelings—whoa, whoa, whoa, feelings." An interesting combination of words. Most of us ride a crisis, pulling the reins on our feelings, hoping somehow to stop them so that the pain will go away.

That was my initial reaction to my own crisis.

That March Ann brought me the box in which she kept her hair ribbons. Shut away in the little box, they had become tangled and knotted together. "Will you separate them?" she asked. As I began to sift and sort the jumble of colors, it occurred to me that this was the very work I needed to do with my own tangled feelings. I needed to open the box and sort.

Like most crises, the midlife trial is a complexity of feelings, a delicate knotting that has to be untied. One of the first strands of feeling that I isolated was a vague sense of grieving and loss. With the breakdown of false selves—what Fritz Kunkel referred to as the "Seeming-Self"[11]—came the fear that the earth under my feet was melting away. Then what? I wondered. It was an empty feeling, an odd kind of mourning.

I felt inward pressure to change, yet I also felt pressure to remain the same. I got anxious over the way my old identity was losing its contours. A part of me wanted to shore it up as a child would pat a crumbling creation in a sandbox. Another part wanted to shed the old identity too quickly. No more Little Girl with a Curl, no more Little Red Hen, no more Tin Woodman. Peel them off like skin. I want out!

Walking inside "the ragged meadow of my soul,"[12] as e. e. cummings so perfectly described it, I met an expanded reality of who I was. Some of it glittered like gemstones, but not all of it was shiny. I treaded shadow places; and there were deep fissures of suffering as I faced realities, ego wants, illusions. One day I said to my counselor, "Surely one of the hardest things in life is learning not to kid ourselves."

"Maybe it's the hardest of all," he said with a smile.

Maybe.

Another strand of feeling was twined around my marriage. Some days I stared painfully into my husband's face, knowing that the vitality had gone out of our relationship. Some days the marriage felt like an empty commitment, a hollowed-out shell that I couldn't figure out how to fill. Somewhere along the way the tide had shifted.

Perhaps it boiled down to the fact that old ways of relating to one another simply weren't adequate. My inner growth propelled me to be my own "I"—to be an authentic woman who was contained in herself, who chose and determined and handled her life from her own genuine spiritual center. Yet at the same time I needed a deeper "we" in our relationship, a sense of journeying together inside. Where was the intimacy that comes when you open your soul and allow the deepest and tenderest of things to flow between you? I needed the sort of honest communion that happens when souls truly meet.

But how do you renegotiate the matrix of a marriage after eighteen years? How do you knit new and deeper cords of intimacy against a backdrop of autonomy and individual personhood? Those are the questions of a midlife marriage. With them can come awe-ful feelings of being trapped, of hopelessness.

A crisis of soul draws up a sense of being caught in in-between-ness, in the "middle space between being able to say 'I am' in a new way and yet wanting to run away from it. We are caught between the 'now' and the 'not-yet' of our identity," notes Alan Jones.[13] In-between was exactly how I felt.

Jung compared this feeling of in-betweenness to being "suspended in mid-air."[14] But I think St. John of the Cross painted the best word picture when he called the in-between experience a "dark night of the soul." He wrote, "David, one who also had experience of this trial, refers to it very clearly in one of the psalms: *I was very afflicted and humbled; I roared with the groaning of the heart*" (his italics).[15]

At my darkest moments it *did* feel as if my heart was groaning. As I write about those terrible sounds, I do so with that odd kind of trepidation that comes from being human in public. Recently I received a letter from a reader who was "surprised at me" because I'd written an article expressing some of these midlife feelings. "Christians shouldn't feel that way," she said. (The implication was pretty obvious.) But the truth is Christians have all kinds of feelings. Their hearts groan in many ways. And frankly, I believe we'll all be better off when we take off our religious masks and become more human. Then we can get on with what really matters—the act of cupping our ears to one another's hearts with compassion.

I have a quote propped beside my computer as I write. It comforts me. "To accept the dark night is to accept being human. . . .It is to accept being who I am. This is holiness."[16]

EXPRESSING THE CLIMATE OF YOUR SOUL

Along with sifting and sorting crisis feelings comes the equally important task of expressing them. In my waiting I found the time and space to give expression to the climate of my soul.

I spent time writing my feelings in my journal. I spoke them to my counselor. I prayed them. I dreamed them. I danced them. I drew them. We each need to find our own unique ways of giving expression to the storm inside us.

We seem to know the value of finding a caring person to listen to our feelings; we understand how helpful it can be to write feelings down. But few of us seem to know the healing that can come from expressing our feelings through symbols.

Symbols are the language of the soul. Because they give us a way to communicate with the soul, they open doors for transformation. Unfortunately, symbolism has become a foreign language for many. Theologian Paul Tillich believed that Protestants were particularly in grave danger of literalizing or impoverishing their symbols. Along with Jung, he called Christians to a revitalization of their inner lives through the recovery of symbols.

Jesus also believed in the spiritual power available within symbols. I am the vine; I am the door; this bread is my body; this wine is my blood: with these words he was creating symbols—images that point to much deeper realities—and giving us a way to contact those realities.

Participating with symbols allows their deeper meaning to wrap around us and penetrate us. Through them, what is lost and unutterable inside us becomes real and accessible. "As the mind explores the symbol it is led to ideas that lie beyond the grasp of reason," wrote Jung.[7]

When I came upon the cocoon in the tree, I stumbled upon the healing power of personal symbols. To discover a symbol means allowing yourself to be grasped by it when it presents itself. For instance, not long after reading the story of Jonah, I was flipping through a catalog and came upon a medieval print of Jonah descending into the whale amid a storming sea. (Another one of those inexplicable "coincidences.") I cut it out, framed it, and hung it on a wall of my study. I had only to glance at it to know what was inside me. The picture embodied an almost inexpressible sentiment floating within me, some beautiful ache and daring hope that I could scarcely articulate. The image made sense of my pain and enfolded me with Presence. Like the cocoon, it became part of the story of my soul.

The picture of the night sea journey, the cocoon, the encased butterflies on my desk, the charcoal sketches of the flapping tent and the homebaked bread—all these, and other images—helped me express the flood of sensations I felt and release the spiritual energy needed to transform them. They were ways of creating a story for myself to live in—a story that began to hold me up like a pair of arms. My symbols mirrored my feelings of dark and light, descent and ascent—images of hope and transformation. Each one seemed to clear a deeper path inside, one that would eventually take me to the other side of my anguish.

PATHOS AND JOY

"Soul-making," wrote philosopher and educator Jean Houston, "is not necessarily a happy thing. Crucial parts of it are not. It almost always involves a painful excursion into pathos wherein the anguish is enormous. . . ."[18]

One day at my desk, feeling the intensity of my own "excursion into pathos," I stared at the cocoon still hanging in my African violets. I felt acutely aware that I was in the passage of separation. I wondered what had compelled the caterpillar to detach from its old larval life and create the chrysalis. Was it responding to an inner voice of change and uprising? Was there a pressing, even painful, sense of the "fullness of time" that made itself known in the creature?

The phone rang, breaking into my thoughts. I picked up the receiver to find Sandy on the other end. Still pondering my questions, I asked him, "How does a caterpillar know it's time to spin a cocoon?"

There was a pause as he waited for the punchline. "I give up," he said. "How *does* a caterpillar know it's time to spin a cocoon?"

I laughed so hard that the dogs, who'd been napping in the kitchen, came to the door of my study and cocked their beagle faces at me. It felt good to laugh.

Hanging up, I was reminded that laughter is soulmaking too, that no matter how dark and serious a crisis seems, I shouldn't abandon my joy. That small human moment on the phone caused me to consider the paradox of pathos and joy in the midst of crisis. Could they coexist?

I remembered that when Ann was four, she tugged on my skirt for attention and asked, "Mama, does God laugh?" God *laugh?* The idea had never entered my head. (I suppose that's one reason we have children: to make us think of inexplicable things.) "Why do you ask?" I said to her.

"Because I think I heard him today," she said.

I gathered her into my arms. "Yes, of course God laughs," I whispered. Maybe that's what life is, I thought: God laughing, God rejoicing.

Eckhart wrote that God laughed into our soul, bringing us joy. He also believed that God suffered.[19] I had no problem with his suffering. It seemed to me that many times when I was crying, I heard God crying too. Perhaps, like Ann, I needed to listen to God laughing.

I once saw a painting of Christ laughing. It touched me deeply. The "man of sorrows" was also the laughing Christ—a man in touch with both the ground of creative suffering and the ground of deep gladness. The most endearing verse in the Bible, to me, is "Jesus wept." He knew about tears and pain, yet he also exulted in the festival of being fully alive.

Standing as I was, in the passage of crisis and separation, I needed to grasp the paradox that while soulmaking can be fraught with tears, it doesn't require the abandonment of joy. After all, nothing is so painful that laughter can't shimmer through it now and then.

I thought back to when Sandy's father died. I was nine months pregnant with our first child—"great with child," as the Bible says. Very. (People were always asking me if I was expecting twins.) At the funeral home the family gathered to pay their respects at the casket. I had been sitting in a low chair. The others waited as I struggled to get to my feet. Someone said later that it looked as if I had banana peelings under my shoes and a watermelon in my lap. Finally not one but two people came to hoist me up. My grieving mother-in-law began to laugh. She said, "You've reminded me that there's still joy in life."

In the crisis we need to hang onto God's little jokes, to those priceless moments when something round with pleasure bounces upon us. We need to hold onto the celebration of becoming, to the bliss that wells up from the deeper places we're tapping.

SPIRITUAL EQUINOX

As I climbed into bed on the eve of the spring equinox, a soft rain was falling. The storm that had seized the backyard earlier in the day had gone, leaving its imprint on torn limbs and battered shrubs—an equinoctial gale, the weatherman had called it. He commented that at the spring equinox, when the sun moves over the equator, the pattern of warm and cold air masses sometimes changes, stirring up the atmosphere. Storms happen.

That seems to be the way of the universe, inner and outer. Crossing spiritual meridians stirs the atmosphere within. People have equinoctial storms too. We need to accept them as part of the crossing over to a new season.

I looked at the clock. Nearly 11:00 P.M. The equinox was due to arrive at 4:39 A.M. At that precise moment the sun would cross the equator and spring would arrive. Afterward, the nights would be shorter and the days would be longer.

The prospect encouraged me. I thought of the darkness that comes upon us in crisis, the black orbits of pain through which we move. I asked God if there would be a spiritual equinox inside me, a crossing over after which a new season would come and the darkness would gradually begin to wane.

I kissed my husband goodnight and drifted to sleep, listening to the night murmur outside my bedroom window. Later I woke to a room full of shadows. The numbers on the clock read 4:38 A.M.

It took a few seconds for the mystery to register. I had awakened for the spring equinox. I slipped from beneath the blanket and tiptoed to the back door. I stared into the night, my heart pounding. Above me, far beyond the bounds of my comprehension, God was threading the night with spring.

I stood still and let the darkness move inside me too.

CHAPTER 5

Letting Go

I am caterpillar. The leaves I eat taste bitter. But dimly I sense a great change coming. What I offer you humans is my willingness to dissolve and transform. I do that without knowing what the end-result will be.
JOANNA MACY, JOHN SEED, PAT FLEMING, ARNE MOSS

The essence of spirituality is contained in this phrase:
complete and utter abandonment to the will of God.
JEAN-PIERRE DE CAUSSADE

All through March the weather remained unpredictable—a vacillating pattern of light and dark. The sun shone one day; the next it retreated into the clouds.

I vacillated too. One day I wanted to follow my midlife crisis to a new place, to separate from old selves and graduate into the chrysalis. The next day I wanted to retreat.

The passage of separation is very much like the fickle days of early spring. Moving through it, we vacillate unpredictably between dark and light, fallowness and growth, clinging and letting go.

We have within us a deep longing to grow and become a new creature, but we possess an equally strong compulsion to remain the same—to burrow down in our safe, secure places. The truth is that we are a patchwork of light and dark, torn between what Quaker writer Thomas Kelly called "the enhancement of our own little selves" and "the God-possessed will."[1]

Shifting from a self-centered focus to a more God-centered focus is terribly hard. I think we've gone wrong by assuming that such a radical movement can be achieved simply by setting our jaw and saying one or two prayers of relinquishment.

Letting go isn't one step but many. It's a winding, spiraling process that happens on deep levels. And we must begin at the beginning: by confronting our ambivalence.

THE DIAPAUSE

One day Sandy came home from work with a book on butterflies. He was grinning. "Maybe you can discover how a caterpillar knows it's time to spin a cocoon," he said (referring to the question I'd asked him on the phone that day—the one he'd mistaken for a riddle).

That night I sat in the den and read about the mysterious process of metamorphosis. The most surprising thing I discovered is that caterpillars don't yield themselves to the cocoon at the same rate. When the moment to spin the chrysalis arrives, some of them actually resist and cling to their larval life. They put off entering the cocoon until the following spring, postponing their transformation a year or more. This state of clinging has a name; it's called the "diapause."

I looked up from the book with a smile. Well, what do you know, I thought. All God's creatures have trouble letting go.

There's a natural diapause in the human journey of transformation—a time when we hold onto the self we know. It seems that at the moment of our greatest possibility, a desperate clinging rises up in us. We make a valiant attempt to "save" our old life. In the words of Daniel Day Williams: "We fear it is all we have. Even its sufferings are familiar and we clutch them because their very familiarity is comforting. . . . Yet so long as we aim at the maintenance of this present self, as we now conceive it, we cannot enter the larger selfhood which is pressing for life."[2]

Thinking about the diapause as I read about caterpillars (and contemplated humans) prompted a barrage of questions: Am I in a spiritual diapause? What's behind all my clinging? Am I trying to save my old self? Do I fear the cocoon because I don't know what might emerge? Am I afraid of change?

These questions caused me to go to a nearby bookshelf and pull out a book that I'd treasured in a special way since childhood: an early edition of Lewis Carroll's *Alice's Adventures in Wonderland*. During times of change in my life, I often think of this book. I took it back to my chair and turned the pages. It evoked a memory in me so vivid that I could recall every feeling, every contour, every color of it.

I was ten, lying in the summer shadows beneath the mimosa tree outside my bedroom window. I was reading my new book, *Alice's Adventures in Wonderland*. I remember my mother's sheets nearby on the backyard clothesline, the hum of a lawnmower in our neighbor's yard, the warmth of my dog, Ginger, sleeping against my legs. I remember the curving lines of the tree and the low swish of wind that made the pink blossoms turn loose and fall. I remember how I used the blossoms to mark the pages in my book. (They always reminded me of the pink tassels that hung from the window shades in my grandmother's parlor.)

All day I read, living the mystery of Alice—especially the way she kept changing from one form and size to another. It was a development that alarmed me almost as much as it did Alice. She would grow tall as a tree, then shrink so much that she could fit through a keyhole. At one point she grew so much that her head pressed against the ceiling of the room and her elbows pushed through the window. Frightened that she would grow right through the roof, she shrank herself down to three inches.

My edition had a picture of miniature Alice peeping over the edge of a mushroom at a smug, hookah-smoking caterpillar. She explained to the caterpillar how frightful it had been for her to undergo all these changes, but he didn't seem to understand. So she said to him, "When you have to turn into a chrysalis—you will someday, you know—and then after that into a butterfly, I should think you'll feel it a little queer, won't you?"

"Not a bit," said the caterpillar.

"All I know is, it would feel very queer to *me*," Alice said.[3]

I stopped reading and lay in the soft shade of the tree, a child who had inadvertently stumbled upon the uncertainty of life, the inevitability of change. Nothing stays the same, I thought, with a queer feeling in my stomach.

Right then I knew that I would grow up and leave that tree. I would say goodbye to my dog, Ginger, to my grandmother's parlor, and to my mother's clean white sheets floating across summer days. In that moment something of my innocence evaporated into the sunlight.

Years later, while packing for college—eager to leave but wanting to stay—I picked up my copy of *Alice's Adventures in Wonderland*, wondering whether to pack it. I sat on my bed and opened it. Tucked between two pages was a crisply dried mimosa blossom—a lost sprinkling of my childhood. Tears sprang to my eyes. It's true, I thought: nothing stays the same. We change forms. We let go and leave the old behind.

I packed the book. Now, in midlife, I held it on my lap.

And once again I was Alice peeping over the edge of a mushroom at the caterpillar, frightened and bewildered by all the change. I was afraid of growing through the roof. I wanted to shrink to three inches tall.

CLINGING

One morning in my study I looked up the word *clinging*. I discovered that it comes from the Anglo-Saxon word *clingan*, which means "shrink." Sure enough, an undeniable connection exists between clinging and shrinking.

One year I decided to plant English ivy as a border around my flower garden. I dipped the small vines in some pH-balanced enzyme powder and planted them around the flowers. Some weeks later the ivy had grown into a small jungle, clinging around the flower stems and causing the blooms to shrink and shrivel. Standing over my flowers, I understood the deadly effect of clinging.

Now I was beginning to understand its effect on the spiritual life. Clinging creates a shrinking within the soul, a shrinking of possibility and growth.

When we're caught in the diapause, we're desperate to shrink away from change. Like Alice, when the growing season comes and our head and elbows begin to press against the small inner rooms in which we've lived, we want to shrink ourselves. The need to cling to "how it was" can be overpowering.

THE STAGES OF LETTING GO

We try and try to let go, only to find ourselves clinging again. So what do we do? We begin by recognizing the reality of our diapause, the naturalness as well as the power of it.

Then we enter the relinquishment process. Thomas Kelly wrote, "The will must be subjected bit by bit, piecemeal and progressively, to the divine Will."[4]

Kelly spoke of four steps in the process of self-abandonment. First, pry open your eyes to the "flaming vision of the wonder of such a life." Second, begin where you are and begin now. Third, if you stumble and "assert your old proud self" (and you will), don't waste a lot of time with regret and self-accusation. Just begin again. These three steps involve self-initiatives, things we're more or less able to control and do ourselves.

The fourth step, however, moves in a completely different direction: "Don't grit your teeth and clench your fists and say, 'I will! I will!' Relax. Take hands off. Submit yourselves to God....Let life be willed through you."[5]

I read the passage several times. Relax? Take hands off? Submit the process to God? And pray tell, what does it mean to "let life be willed through you"? Was there a shift in the process of letting go from the active to the passive?

This all intrigued me a great deal. Exploring further, I found that Thomas Merton suggested that there are two levels to the process of abandoning self-will and surrendering fully to God. First, there is the active work we do with the conscious, surface attachments in our life—those patterns we recognize and can campaign against. He wrote that to let go of these "you pray and suffer and hang on and give things up and hope and sweat."[6] This seemed to correspond to Kelly's first three steps. At this level we approach letting go the active way, through self-initiatives, will, and work. We begin and begin again. By our own sweat and effort we work to let go of attachments that are mainly on the surface.

The second level deals with deeper, more unconscious patterns— what Merton called our "secret attachments." To uproot these he cautioned that "we need to leave the initiative in the hands of God working in our souls either directly in the night of aridity and suffering, or through events and other men."[7]

Merton suggested that on this level we shift to a different way of letting go—one that has a curious similarity to Kelly's fourth step. Here the approach becomes more mysterious. We let go our letting go. We stop struggling, stop saying, "I *will* let go, I will, I will." Instead, having done all we can, we allow God to work directly on the more secret and deeply ingrained attachments we have to self. We allow God to release us *through the experiences, encounters, and events* that come to us.

It suddenly made sense to me why our letting go so often fails. We remain at the first level. As Merton wrote,

> This is where so many holy people break down. . . . As soon as they reach the point where they can no longer see the way and guide themselves by their own light, they refuse to go any further. . . . It is in this darkness that we find true liberty. It is in this abandonment that we are made strong. This is the night that empties us.[8]

You and I have lived on the first level. Perhaps there has to be a phase of active praying, hanging on, turning loose, sweating, trying, and trying again. But the question we should ask is, Have we stopped there? I wondered, had I?

In waiting we're also called to enter the second level: the night that empties us of our clinging. We're called to let go even our letting go. We need to quit forcing things and enter the darkness of true liberty, where we give up self-efforts and allow God to intercede and draw us to our moment of readiness.

UNCURLING THE FINGERS

One winter night years ago I slipped into Ann's room to make sure she was covered. (She's a notorious blanket kicker.) The nightlight glowed through the organdy ruffle of her canopied bed, where she lay fast asleep. Just as I suspected, her blanket was at the foot of the bed. As I drew it to her chin, I noticed that she clutched a half-eaten grape lollipop—one that her grandmother had given her on her birthday. It was an all-day sucker that had turned into a two-day affair. Now it had made a sticky purple splotch on her pillowcase, and a few strands of her hair were stuck to it. Disgusting.

Why didn't she get rid of this before going to bed, I thought. Her little fingers still clung tightly to the stick, and I had to pry them off one by one. Once it was free, I tossed the grape sucker in the trash.

The next morning she confronted me in a blaze of righteous indignation. "But it was *mine*, and I wasn't ready to throw it away!" She was right, of course. I hadn't even asked her permission. I ended up buying her another sucker, and we went through the whole process again.

One of the lessons that remained with me from that experience is that when it comes to letting go, we have to arrive at a moment of genuine readiness.

When we enter Merton's second level of surrender to God we don't use force to pry our clinging fingers away; nor does God. Rather, granting infinite, loving freedom, God offers us the experiences, events, and encounters that help us find the courage to open them ourselves, with gentleness.

THE COURAGE TO BE

"In human beings courage is necessary to make being and becoming possible," wrote Rollo May.[9] It takes courage to let go and yield yourself to the changes that take place in the chrysalis. It takes courage to become who you are. Merton said that it was cowardice that kept us "double-minded" and hesitating between the world of self and God.

The opposite of courage isn't only fear but security. One day at church the sermon was on Jesus' words to the rich young man who asked him how to inherit eternal life. "Go, sell what you have,... and come follow me," Jesus advised him (Mark 10:21). When I heard that line I felt "spoken to." Go, sell your security. Stop clinging. Let go and launch out into the deep of yourself. This is what it means to tap life eternal.

The minister that Sunday said that security was a denial of life. I suppose that's true in the sense that total security eliminates all risk. And where there's no risk, there's no becoming; and where there's no becoming, there's no real life. The real spiritual sojourners—the ones who touch the edges of life as well as the center—are people who risk, who let go.

Years ago I volunteered at a shelter for abused children. One day I met Billy, a boy with spiky brown hair and pale brows to match his pale face. The only life in him was a thirsty look in the half-moons of his eyes. He'd been horribly wounded and was reluctant to go beyond the security he'd found in his room. The day of the Christmas party he shrank against the pillow on his bed and refused to leave his room. "But aren't you coming to the party?" I asked. He shook his head.

"*Sure* you are," said the volunteer beside me. "All you need is to put on your courage skin."

His pale brows went up, as did mine. The thirsty look in his eyes seemed to drink in the possibility. "Okay," he finally said. While I watched, she helped him don an imaginary suit of "courage skin," and off he went to the party, willing to risk going beyond secure places. Go, sell all you have, Jesus said, and follow me into life. We have to risk everything in order to gain everything. In his small way, that's what Billy was doing.

Sometimes, when I'm overwhelmed by the challenge of living authentically, living the deeper self in me, I remember Billy and take heart.

Courage comes from the French word *coeur*, which means "heart." In order to travel from clinging to letting go, we have to "take heart." The heart is the seat of the will. This is the place God awakens, the place where the gentle uprooting takes place.

One day I picked up a pencil and scribbled a prayer.

To be fully human, fully myself,
To accept all that I am, all that you envision,
This is my prayer.
Walk with me out to the rim of life,
Beyond security.
Take me to the exquisite edge of courage
And release me to become.

Recognizing that letting go is a piecemeal process and that I needed now to come to my moment of readiness in God's time and way, I decided to let go of letting go and wait on God to work within me. I wanted to stand back and let God give me the experiences, encounters, and events I needed to awaken my courage.

Looking back, I'm aware of several experiences that sifted together to bring me quietly to the place of letting go. They had the effect of slowly and gently uncurling my grip, finger by finger.

Let It Be

The first happened while I was poking around the attic looking for a picture frame. I opened a box and found a bundle of Christmas cards we'd received in 1975. (It's a mystery to me why I keep Christmas cards more than ten years. I'm either too sentimental or a ridiculous pack rat; I'm not sure which.)

I sat down under the exposed lightbulb dangling from the rafter and looked through them. Halfway through I found a card that had meant a great deal to me that year.

I was seven months pregnant that Christmas. There were days when I thought that I would be the first woman in history to stay pregnant her entire life. I was terribly tired of waiting. I ached to hold my baby in my arms; I yearned to count her toes, not to mention *see* my own. The days seemed to drag by, and I was miserable.

That's when the card came. On the front was Mary, great with child, the universal Lady in Waiting. And inside were the words, "Let it be." I felt a sudden kinship with her; I felt that she had come to tell me how to wait through my pregnancy. Don't fret so, the card seemed to say. You can't control the life in you. It grows and emerges in its own time. Be patient and nurture it with all your love and attentiveness. Be still and cooperate with the mystery God is unfolding in you. *Let it be*.

"Let it be to me according to your word" (Luke 1:38). Those were the words Mary spoke to the angel when he announced to her that she would give birth to God's son, the words that ushered her into the gestation of divinity and the experience of waiting. With them, she let go of her own will and the security of her old way of life and yielded to the purposes of God.

Now, years later in the attic, I held the Christmas card in my hands with the feeling that I was *supposed* to be in the attic at that very moment, finding the card and discovering Mary's words once again. I sensed that the words "let it be" were about to take up residence in me and sing their sacred little aria of letting go.

I said them out loud, whispered them into the golden haze of the attic. "Let it be..." Such beautiful words. They show us how to begin our own incarnation journey. We're being asked to nurture the implanted seed of the divine nature and bring it forth in our souls. Each of us is Mary.

I thought of that often-ignored verse in 2 Peter that speaks of God's "precious and very great promise" that we could "become partakers of the divine nature" (2 Peter 1:4). Dear God, have any of us ever, ever *truly* taken this in? I wondered.

What if we gave this verse more attention? Would more of us be making the incarnation journey? Would we be paying more attention to providing the womb—the dark stillness and receptivity necessary for the birth of the inner Christ-self: the True Self?

Not so long ago I visited Springbank Retreat Center, tucked among the mossy live oaks in the low country of South Carolina. Just inside the door was a picture of the pregnant Madonna. Beside the picture were these words: "This image represents each person who is trying to birth the Real Self, the *Imago Dei* that is taking shape within. For that conception to move to its fullness, we all need time to be quiet, to be reflective, to be centered in our deep places."

In other words, we need time to wait.

The experience in the attic caused me to think of Mary's letting go, and of how three simple words opened the way into waiting and birthing. That's where letting go always leads. "The fruit of letting go is birth," wrote Eckhart.[10]

As I climbed down the ladder, clutching the Christmas card, my pregnant soul wanted to surrender as Mary had done. The words "let it be" floated inside me with new-found peace.

Handing Yourself Over

Not long after that attic experience I came upon an event in the Bible that also had the effect of moving me closer to letting go: Jesus' arrest in Gethsemane. Reflecting on it, Henri Nouwen wrote,

> The central word in the story of Jesus' arrest is one I never thought much about. It is 'to be handed over.' Judas handed Jesus over. . . . The remarkable thing is that the same word is used not only for Judas but also for God. God did not spare Jesus, but handed him over to benefit us all. (See Rom. 8:32.) So this word, 'to be handed over,' plays a central role in the life of Jesus. Indeed, this drama of being handed over divides the life of Jesus radically in two.[11]

Nouwen pointed out that the first part of Jesus' life is marked by activity; the second, by waiting. In the first part Jesus was teaching, healing, going from town to town, taking the initiative, and doing things. But after he was handed over, "he becomes the one to whom things are being done."[12]

On being handed over Jesus underwent a switch to a receiving mode. He didn't fight against the suffering to come, the incredible tensions he knew he had to endure. He let go and entered his passion—the passive endurance of the waiting experience. It was striking to me to find that the most crucial part of Jesus' life came in his waiting. How odd that in the holy stretch of waiting we discover God's deepest purposes!

I realized that both waiting and the life-giving transformation that came out of it began for Jesus at the very point when he handed himself over, just as they begin for us when we hand ourselves over. We're meant to live the Christ-life, including his waiting and his passion. We're meant to hand ourselves over so that we can wait our own wait, hold our own tensions, enter our own suffering, emerge from our own tomb and know aliveness for the first time.

This new way of thinking about and dwelling in Jesus' passion unlocked new courage in me. I felt myself drawn into the deeper experience of waiting, of "handing myself over," even though at times I seemed to be doing so only in bits and pieces.

"The Whole Point Is to Let Go"

During my visit to the Abbey of Gethsemani earlier that winter, I'd walked through the woods to Merton's hermitage with my husband and Brother Anthony.

It's hard to describe how excited I was to be there. Merton's works had meant much to me, and I'd been irresistibly drawn to the still beauty of monasteries ever since I'd made my first monastic retreat at St. Meinrad Archabbey in Indiana many years earlier. Sometimes people ask me what a "nice Protestant girl" like me sees in those places. I smile and tell them that I simply can't help it; after all, my maiden name is Monk. But the truth is I go there because monasteries are one of the last examples on earth of living for God and God alone and focusing one's whole life around the rhythms of prayer. I believe that the monastic community has something to teach me, and I always come away graced.

Walking through the woods that day, I thought about these things, wondering how God would come to me this time. We talked a bit about the spiritual life as we wound our way through the pines. When we reached the hermitage, Brother Anthony paused beside a wagon wheel that was propped against a cross in the frontyard. "You know, the whole purpose is to let go," he said, "to be still, like this wheel, and let the action be done from God's side. That's what opens us to the deep Center."

For a silent moment we all stared at the wagon wheel while time deepened and turned golden around us. Overhead in a pine tree a crow cawed out its presence. I lifted my eyes and gazed at it.

One evening soon after, Sandy and I fell into a conversation about those moments—about Brother Anthony's words and the crow in the tree. Sandy said, "You know what came to mind when I saw that crow perched over us? I thought of the Native American proverb about the eagle and the crow in each of us. The eagle flies here, there, and everywhere, following the wild currents of the wind. But the crow sits serenely among the corn stalks and waits."

I liked that proverb; it fit well with Brother Anthony's words that day: "The whole purpose is to let go." I let them replay in my mind, over and over. I heard them on a deeper level than I had before. It was as if something inside me were "released." I wanted to let go and enter the deep stillness that Brother Anthony had pointed out to us.

In the very same hermitage I'd visited, Merton had once written this prayer: "You have willed to see me more really as I am. For the sinful self is not my real self, it is not the self You have wanted for me, only the self I have wanted for myself. *And I no longer want this false self.*"[13] How I understood! The question is whether to follow the wild current of one's own heart or to sit serenely in God's stillness.

Letting go is like releasing a tight spring at the core of yourself, one you've spent your whole life winding and maintaining. When you let go, you grow still and silent. You learn to sit among the cornstalks and wait with God.

Once I led a small group of college students in a creative worship experience. I gave each one a piece of kite string, asked them to shape it into something that symbolized where they were in their spiritual journey, and share their symbol with the group. One girl held up her string with a knot tied at the end. She said, "Lately things have been going all wrong. Nothing is working. I feel like I'm at the end of my rope, but I've tied a knot in it and am holding on."

We continued around the circle. Another girl's string looked the same as it did when I gave it to her. "I came to the end of my rope too, but I didn't tie a knot; I decided to let go and drop. The surprising thing is that God caught me."

I felt that I was the one being led into worship. This girl's response was the one that Brother Anthony had spoken about: giving up our desperate striving to hold on, letting go into still-ness—into God, whose arms are always underneath.

Die and Become

As March drew to a close, I had a dream. The next morning I recorded it in my journal:

I'm walking through a mazelike cavern full of twists and turns. As I move along, I come upon a man carving something on a large wooden beam. I pause and look at him, then start to walk on. As I do so, he lets the beam fall across my path like a gate. I see the words he's carved in the wood. They say, "Die and become." I want to continue on my way, but I can't get around the beam.

This dream suggested to me that becoming more whole is an experience of dying that I simply couldn't get around. "Those who participate in change must participate in death," wrote Elizabeth O'Conner.[14]

I felt a sharpening in my willingness to let my false, egoistic patterns pass away—all the things I clung to for meaning, success, security, and validation. I knew that these patterns included not only the images I had of myself but the ones others had of me. I needed to let them die.

St. Teresa of Avila once compared the soul to a silkworm. She wrote,

> It is necessary for the silkworm to die. Let's be quick to do this work and weave this little cocoon....Let it die; let this silkworm die, as it does in completing what it was created to do....A little white butterfly comes forth. Oh, greatness of God!...Truly I tell you that the soul doesn't recognize itself.[15]

To "let the silkworm die" we have to keep before us the image of the little white butterfly, as the caterpillars Stripe and Yellow discover. Yellow came upon a gray-haired caterpillar who told her about becoming a butterfly. "But how do you become one?" she asked.

"You must want to fly so much that you are willing to give up being a caterpillar," he said.

"You mean to *die?*" asked Yellow.

"Yes and no," he answered. "What *looks* like you will die but what's *really* you will still live."[16]

What's *really* you and I. Isn't that what matters most?

If you lose your life for my sake, you will find it, Jesus said (Matt. 10:39). Die and become. Could that be the fundamental theme of the New Testament?

Last summer I sat in a lounge chair on a South Carolina beach watching a seagull peck at the sand. Soon a little boy around four years old crept up behind the bird. The gull fluttered away and the child ran after him, flapping his arms in imitation.

It was exactly what my now-sixteen-year-old son used to do when he was small. While everyone else was in the surf, he stalked seagulls down the beach (with me tagging behind him). Now it came to me with a stab of pain that that little boy of mine was gone forever. So was his mother.

I walked down to the water and stood ankle-deep in the ocean. A wave rolled by, folding across the surface. It spread into a thin veil decorated with scraps of lacy foam. As the wave whisked back into the sea, the suction pulled the sand out from under my feet. I had the feeling that I was going to topple over, that everything was being tugged away. Nothing stays the same, those moments said to me. In one year my son would be leaving home for college, just as I had that day I sat on my bed and found the mimosa blossom inside *Alice's Adventures in Wonderland*. I would have to die to the old roles and images of myself in relation to him. I couldn't tag behind him through life.

The waves rolled in and out full of whispers. *Die and become. Die and become.* In ways large and small we must cooperate with the inevitability of change.

"What kind of music plays in your heart when you learn that part of loving is knowing when to allow another to walk away?" asks Alan Jones.[17] I'll tell you what kind: the sweet and painful little aria "let it be."

That spring the words "die and become" blended with the words "let it be." They blended with the images of Jesus handing himself over and of the crow in the tree. In such ways God draws us, inch by inch, prayer by prayer, wave by wave washing over us, until we finally open our hands once and for all.

THE BRIDGE

In the middle of spring I traveled to northern California to speak. While I was there, I ventured alone one afternoon into a forest of redwoods. The air was cool and full of mist as I walked a trail of angular hills and precipices that plunged below me. I passed tiny white butterflies moving in the dimness.

Above me the trees blotted out the sky except for dusty beams of light lancing through the leaves. Feeling at home in the checkered light, I inched down a hill. Hearing the sound of water rushing in a creek, I stopped. A long wooden bridge spanned a chasm just before me. The creek—swathed in mist, almost floating in mist—splashed far below.

I felt as if I'd come to the brink of all my prayers and searching. Letting go is like crossing a bridge, I thought. I walked to the edge of it. "'When you have to turn into a chrysalis...I should think you'll feel it a little queer, won't you?' Alice asked."

My legs felt weak as I started over the bridge. In my heart I knew that this was more than a stroll through a pretty scene. It was my own ritual of letting go. Something told me that I had come to my moment of readiness.

I told God that walking the bridge was my way of expressing the movement inside me, a way of letting go of self-will, egoistic ways, culturally ingrained images, things that were past, old illusions, crumbled myths, fears, and lies.

My letting go wasn't complete and perfect. I know that. The process continues on in us forever, I suppose. But I sensed that this was my moment to *express* the shifting I felt inside. It was the beginning of leaving behind the first half of my life and those ways of living it that no longer worked. What I was walking toward, I had no idea.

Halfway across the bridge I stopped and stared down into the ravine. There was that awful ache again. Letting go can be so wrenching. There were huge weights in my shoes even then.

I looked across the bridge, wanting to turn around and go back. *Please, God.* I stared at my feet. When I finally looked up, I saw one of those plentiful white butterflies dipping and flying about on the other side of the bridge. I fixed my eyes on it and walked across. God gives us the courage one way or the other, if only we would see it.

On the other side of the bridge I sat down under a redwood, feeling spent but oddly light. The lightness welled up in me and became laughter that traveled among the trees. And I thought about that old saying: "When the heart weeps for what it has lost, / The spirit laughs for what it has found."

I told God, "Thank you, thank you, thank you!" Then I sat quietly and wondered what it must be like to spin a cocoon.

PASSAGE OF
TRANSFORMATION

CHAPTER 6

Concentrated Stillness

There should always be more waiting than striving in a Christian's prayer.

EVELYN UNDERHILL

Nothing in all creation is so like God as stillness.

MEISTER ECKHART

I came home from the redwoods of California ready to learn the art of spinning a chrysalis. But where would I begin? What do we humans know about creating a cocoon for spiritual transformation? How do we fashion an environment in which we become stripped and stilled, in which the ego patterns of a lifetime begin to move away from the center and our innermost spiritual life is reconstellated? How do we create the threads that hold us in the painful, uncertain, solitary darkness of waiting—and hold us not only *in* the waiting but *through* the waiting?

Those were the questions I asked myself. Finding answers was made more difficult by the fact that so little attention is paid in our culture to the value of waiting. I could find no books about the process of the waiting journey, no blueprints for a chrysalis, no classes on how to wait. One evening I heard Professor James Fowler of Candler School of Theology at Emory University lecture. He lamented, "We are always wanting to put people on escalators to go to the next stage of faith as quickly as possible." The comment struck me as true; yet if Christianity is geared to escalator spirituality rather than the spirituality of the cocoon, where would I look for guidance in spinning a chrysalis?

Well, I said to myself, I'll look to God. I'll look within.

I've been impressed with the emphasis that Quakers place on the concept of Christ as one who teaches us from within, of the Holy Spirit as the Inward Guide. What would happen if we took this seriously? What if we turned to the Inward Guide to lead us through our waiting?

Referring to this Guide, Thomas Merton said, "We don't have to rush after it. It was there all the time and if we give it time, it will make itself known to us."[1] In the weeks and months that followed my crossing of the bridge I learned the truth of these words. I learned that there's hardly anything upon which God heaps more grace and guidance than chrysalis making. God dreamed up the idea of the cocoon, and I believe that God invests in the waiting of every creature who enters one. If we're tuned to epiphanies—those guiding flashes of sacred insight—they happen, usually just when we need them most.

When Ann was six, she lost her doll, Cindy. We searched for days. Cindy became a regular part of bedtime prayers. One day, while Ann was eating lunch, she mystified me by laying down her fork, going to the backyard, and crawling under the forsythia bush. There was Cindy. We could only imagine that the dog had dragged her there. "How did you know to look under the forsythia?" I asked. My daughter shrugged. "I just knew it inside," she said. The inner guiding grace. Who can fathom it? But it's there for all of us, especially in the process of waiting and transformation.

Such grace comes, not only through the inner nudge of guidance, but also through the exterior world around us. In fact, when I think of waiting, the last line in Bernanos's *Diary of a Country Priest* frequently comes to my mind: "Grace is everywhere." The statement appalls me at times. But then so many things about God appall me. The immense, unreasonable love for us, the outrageous insistence that in the weak and broken there is divine Presence, the indomitable faith in us as children of hope, to mention a few. But most of all, I'm caught off guard by God's grace-fulness, by a graceful universe, by the grace of the ordinary. We've underestimated the presence of grace among us. We've built up a callus over it with our cynicism and the religious certainties that render us incapable of being surprised.

If we're to wait, we must relearn the extravagance of grace.

A SILHOUETTE OF GRACE

I began to weave my cocoon one foggy night in April. I had just finished a game of Clue with Sandy and the children. Bob had discovered the solution: Miss Scarlett in the library with the knife.

"Outwitted you again!" he teased.

"So you did," I said, but I suspected that he had more or less happened upon the truth by accident.

As the children put away the game, I stood at the patio doors, gazing into the soupy night and thinking how tempting it is to turn waiting into a game of Clue—hurrying as fast as you can through the corridors, searching for clues that will give you the answers you need.

The fog was so thick that I couldn't see the chimneys on my neighbors' roofs, much less the moon or stars. I've always liked the way I feel when it's foggy out, as if God had dropped a veil over me. Fog is very cocoonlike, I thought.

Suddenly I was aware of my soul standing in the dark, in the opaqueness of midlife, unable to do anything but wait. I wanted to pray, to form words and petitions, but there was only the eerie stillness of my heart. The feeling of being unable to pray as I was accustomed to had been with me ever since I'd walked over the bridge in a ritual of letting go.

Why couldn't I pray? *Why?* I stood by the doors, watching the fog, everything in me hushed and unmoving. All at once I caught my reflection in the glass. I saw my posture silhouetted against the darkness. And it came to me in one of those grace-ful moments— one like my daughter had had, when she simply "knew" something inside: *I was seeing myself at prayer.* I *was* praying. My still heart, my silence, the very posture of waiting against a backdrop of darkness was my prayer.

The revelation came as a surprise. And like Bob, I hadn't outwitted a thing. I had *stumbled* into grace.

Those moments held a compelling awareness for me. Making a cocoon and the transformation that goes on inside it involves weaving an environment of prayer, but not the sort of prayer we usually think of. No, this is something mysteriously different. This prayer isn't about talking and doing and thinking. It's about *postures*. Postures of the spirit. It's turning oneself upside down so that everything is emptied out and God can flow in. It's curling up in the fogged spaces of the listening heart, sinking into solitude, wrapping the soul around some little flame of hope that God has ignited. It's sitting on the window sill of the heart, still and watching.

Such interior postures are themselves the prayers that transform, heal, and yield the answers in our waiting. They're the shapes and contours that turn us into a cocoon.

THE SPIRITUAL CREMASTER

A few days later I again picked up the book on butterflies that Sandy had given me. I read that when the caterpillar begins to spin its chrysalis, it forms a spiny little protuberance at the end of its abdomen called the *cremaster*. The cremaster is like a button or patch of Velcro that fastens the pupa in the cocoon and holds it in place. It's the anchor point, the place from which the caterpillar hangs.

My mind whirled to the poetry of T. S. Eliot, who wrote about a still point, a spiritual place where there's no going forward or going backward. A point within us where we're fastened, and around which everything turns. "Except for the point, the still point, there would be no dance," he wrote.[2]

The still point is our cremaster. Without it, there's no dance of transformation. It's the place where all cocoon making starts. We need to find the point in our soul where we go neither forward nor backward but are fastened in our waiting. We need to discover the "protuberance" from which our lives can silently hang and become new.

What *is* this still point? It represents the Center, the quiet core where God's Spirit dwells in us. "Do you not know that...God's Spirit dwells in you?" (1 Cor. 3:16). Sometimes we *don't* seem to know it. Yet in some holy place within us, God lives and moves and has being (2 Cor. 6:16). At this inmost center of our being, a place where we're deeply and profoundly known and loved by God, is the Presence in our midst.

It's here that we attach ourselves to God. But this is also where God attaches to us. Ultimately, the still point is a love meeting, an embrace. Hildegard wrote,

> God hugs you.
> You are encircled
> by the arms
> of the mystery of God.[3]

God's hug. What a wonderful image! That circle is your still point. And you form your cremaster by attaching to this inner place of loving embrace with the Divine.

Almost daily the delicate threads of my cocoon would start to unravel, and I would have to go back and find the inner anchor from which to hang. Our minds can become clogged with the busyness and details of living—things that make us fret and squirm, things that make us run from waiting and the slow greening of our soul. That's when we need to pause and reconnect ourselves to the still point.

There are about as many ways to go about this as there are people. Each human heart approaches the still point in its own unique manner. The capacity that you and I have for creativity when it comes to our own inner becoming is vast and impressive.

I believe in the individuality of each human soul. We're each artists, along with God, in its creation. Meister Eckhart believed that an artist isn't a special kind of person but that each person is a special kind of artist. Think of it; you're your own special kind of artist. Your soul is your canvas, your flute, your poem. And you paint it, play it, and write it as every true artist does—in unique collaboration with God.

This makes for diversity in our approaches to the still point. What then binds those approaches? A deep intent of the whole heart to God. David Steindl-Rast says that anything we do with a whole heart can be prayer.[4] In wholeheartedness, our entire being is united in its aim toward God, toward the deep Center within.

You have found and will find your own ways of doing this. In the mornings of my cocoon days I often found the still point by lighting a candle and watching its silent flame for five or ten minutes, my heart warm and focused on God. Sometimes I paused to reflect on the pictures and symbols in my study—to gaze at Jonah descending into the whale or run my finger over the Christmas card that pictured Mary pregnant with the Christ child. Other times I returned to the still point by taking a few silent minutes to stroll under the stars in the backyard, listen to music, or curl up with my sketch pad. The idea is to still ourselves, to draw ourselves back to the deeper life that flows beneath the surface of our days.

THE PRAYER OF WAITING

Having discovered the cremaster, I began to try to open myself more fully to the postures that create a cocoon. Waiting prayer, as I've already indicated, isn't found on the regular prayer menu. It has little to do with petition and intercession and getting God to fix things (though these can be important kinds of prayers). Waiting prayer is different.

Author and Presbyterian minister Eugene Petersen was quoted in an interview as saying, "The assumption of spirituality is that *always* God is doing something before I know it. So the task is not to get God to do something I think needs to be done, but to become aware of what God is doing so that I can respond to it and participate and take delight in it."[5]

This is the motivation behind waiting prayer. We place ourselves in postures of the heart, in the stillness that enables us to become aware of what God is doing so that we can gradually say yes to it with our whole being.

My phone rang one morning. A friend in New York was calling to tell me about a "momentous breakthrough" in her life. She had spent much of her forty-three years as a Little Red Hen in the career world. Struggling and striving to reach the top rung in her corporation, to excel and prove herself to the point of being a martyr to the cause, she had finally burned out. She'd spent part of the last year, she told me, going through lots of internal crisis.

The more I listened, the more I suspected that she had been slogging about in the same sort of midlife swamp I had. She too had reached the black bottom. She said, "I thought about my life and how I was living it, and I asked myself, Why bother?"

Her question brought back echoes of a passage from Janice Brewi and Anne Brennan's *Mid-life*:

> When, one day in mid-life, one comes to doubt oneself, and all one's relationships and commitments, and when the pain and anxiety of this dragging away of...energy from all that formerly was so life-giving begins to overwhelm, there surfaces the depth question: *Why bother?* Lucky the one who lets that question stand.... That question is a prayer.[6]

Had my friend let that question become a prayer? "What happened then?" I asked her.

"I decided that I needed time," she said. Waiting time, I thought.

"I went away to Maine and walked in the country. As I walked, I begged and pleaded with God to change things. I was as feverish in my prayers as I had been in my career. Then I came upon a spider web that hung between two trees. The spider was still in the midst of spinning it. I can't explain why, but I stopped and watched. It occurred to me that I'd never done anything so irrelevant in my life—or so it seemed."

I smiled. Waiting always feels irrelevant in the beginning.

She went on: "I sat on a stump for the longest time, watching the spider. And you know what? The most beautiful thing happened. This is the way you're supposed to pray, a voice inside me said. Just be quiet and still so that you can begin to see the thing God is already weaving. So that's what I've started to do."

There was silence between us. Then she said, "Funny how something like that can change everything, isn't it?"

Yes, it is. Funny how God strews our paths with little webs of grace that pull us into the prayer of waiting, into healing and rebirth.

My friend had found the prayer of concentrated stillness, an extraordinary and powerful prayer, but one little known to us. By taking on the shapes and postures of this prayer, we become the cocoon. Aligning ourselves—heart, body, mind, and spirit—into unique positions of stillness creates the special environment we need. It creates the waiting season in which we become able to commune with our depths and begin to recover what is lost, heal what is wounded, and become who we truly are.

The prayer of concentrated stillness means taking on three inward postures. They're symbolized in three examples of sitting found in the Bible.

Sitting at Jesus' Feet

One day, while flipping through the New Testament, I came upon the familiar story of Mary and Martha (Luke 10:39). Jesus came to Mary's house for a visit. There was a lot of fuss and flurry in the kitchen, and Mary's sister, Martha, got completely wound up in it and missed the point of everything. Mary, on the other hand, defied a lot of taboos by entering the circle of men who had gathered as disciples around Jesus. The Bible says that she sat at his feet and fixed her listening heart upon him.

As I read the story, an odd thing happened. (The stirring of more grace, I suspect.) I felt tears on my face as I was swept up by the fresh, pure wonder of what Mary had done. I felt drawn to her as if she were my lost sister.

I thought about the daring that she had mustered to break out of expected patterns that confined the deeper contemplative part of her and to position herself as she did. I tried imagining how she looked there—sitting still, watching Christ's face, focusing not only her eyes but her heart on him.

I understood that what I was seeing was the posture of waiting. I was seeing the prayer of the cocoon.

This sitting at the feet of the Divine with an attentive and loving heart is a posture we all long to assume, whether we recognize that longing or not. Our longing for it is deep and universal. What so many people nowadays don't know is that Mary *is* the lost sister. She's the lost and beautiful part within each of us, the contemplative that sits in the divine presence with a fully tuned heart.

I wrote four words across the margin of my Bible: attention of the heart. That seemed to be the aim and the central characteristic of Mary's posture.

"Attention of the heart" is an ancient contemplative phrase that has appeared in the spiritual writings of the Church from the earliest centuries. In *Lost Christianity*, author Jacob Needleman embarks on a quest to find the essence of the Christian experience, much of which he feels has been "lost." The author's search led him to the writings of a tenth-century saint named Simeon, who wrote that attention of the heart is the primary aim of spiritual work—that it guides us to the center of our being, to the heart.

Needleman was struck by the enormity of truth contained in this idea. Here was something viable, he thought—a real bridge toward spiritual change, a means of transforming consciousness so that one could become the deepest and truest self. "This attention *is* prayer," wrote Needleman. "It is that which watches and waits in the night."[7]

I envision attention of the heart as the combination of two interior states: attentiveness and devotion. When Mary sits still in the divine presence, she's a perfectly blended portrait of each.

Attentiveness is vital to waiting. The word *wait* comes from a root word meaning "to watch." Originally to *wait* meant to apply attentiveness or watchfulness throughout a period of time and was a highly regarded experience. To wait on God meant to watch keenly for God's coming. *Watchers* and *waiters* were nearly synonymous.

Unfortunately, much of this meaning has been emptied out of our experience of waiting. These days, the idea of waiting doesn't conjure up the idea of being tuned in as much as it does the idea of being tuned out. We denigrate it to idling.

I came upon one of my daughter's friends standing outside a store one afternoon and asked what she was doing.

"Waiting around," she replied.

"Waiting around?"

"You know, killing time," she said. We need to recover the sacred relationship between waiting and watching. When I was a dating teenager, every time I went out, my mother said, "I'll be waiting up for you!" I knew what that meant. She would be awake, watching for my return, attentive to car lights in the driveway and voices on the porch. Her heart would be focused on me as only a parent's heart can be.

The other attitude inherent in attention of the heart is devotion. Like watchfulness, devotion is always present in genuine waiting.

We don't hear a lot these days about the experience of devotion to God, about cultivating tenderness and passion for the one who made us and sustains us. I wonder sometimes if we haven't banished the way of the heart in favor of the way of the mind, if we emphasize learning *about* God over being *with* God.

Henri Nouwen believes that one of the more demonic ruses around today aims "to make us think of prayer primarily as an activity of the mind that involves above all our intellectual capacities. This prejudice reduces prayer to speaking with God or thinking about God."[8] Prayer isn't strictly a mental activity any more than it's strictly an emotional activity. It's an experience of the *whole* being.

I talk with growing numbers of people for whom life with God has become a pile of dying embers. When we douse the experience of devotion, prayer has a tendency to die out as well. What's happened to the experience of sacred adoration, of sitting and delighting in God's presence in the fiery place of the heart? God created us in order to share the joy of being alive with us, in order to love us and taste our love, to delight in us and enjoy our delight. God wants our hearts.

By far the dearest passage in *The Practice of the Presence of God* comes when Brother Lawrence writes, "My most useful way of relating to God is this simple attention and a real desire for God. Often I find myself attached to God with greater delight than a baby at his mother's breast."[9] Brother Lawrence knew the tender flames of devotion.

As I attempted to take on the posture of Mary at the divine feet, I didn't struggle to set a "quiet time" or do a lot of mental exercises. I simply took time out now and then to sit still and experience attention of the heart. I often sat on the patio in the early morning, listening to the owl that always sang invisibly from a distant tree. Sometimes I sat in the dusk in a near-blizzard of fireflies. Once I got away for a weekend and sat in my stillness for even longer, unbroken spaces of time. Inwardly I fixed my heart on God. I tried to watch, to be attentive, to love and be present to God, creation, my own aliveness, even the holiness of an owl's call.

For me, that's the posture of Mary—the still prayer of waiting that transforms us in unseen ways.

This posture can sustain us through unbearable stretches of waiting. When Bob was in elementary school, I had an after-school PTA meeting in the lunchroom. Bob had ridden his bicycle that day so that he wouldn't have to hang around for the meeting to end. I saw him on his way to the bike rack when I arrived. "Will your meeting be long?" he called.

"It might," I said, "but I'll be home as soon as I can."

When I left the meeting at four o'clock, I practically stumbled over Bob, who was sitting cross-legged on the floor, leaning against the lunchroom door. "I waited for you, Mama!" he said, leaping up.

"But you didn't *have* to wait," I protested.

"I know. I just wanted to. I wanted to give you this." He thrust a crinkled sheet of notebook paper under my nose. On the front was a drawing of an airplane, an uneven row of tulips, and a fat yellow sun. I opened it up to read, "I love you."

I looked down at him, overwhelmed that I could be the object of so much devotion that my son would wait an hour and a half in a deserted school corridor with a love note scrunched in his hand. I pulled him close against me, so close that he said, "I can hear your heart beating against my ear, Mama."

I held him even closer, delighting in my child who was delighting in me. That's what happens when we wait in the posture of Mary. We delight in God, who delights in us.

Maybe it's the mother in me, but I refuse to believe that God, who is like a Mother to us all, doesn't also delight in such watchfulness and devotion—the kind that keeps us waiting even when we don't have to.

When we, like Mary, sit in a pool of divine presence, our hearts full and attentive in the midst of our darkness and pain, we're praying ourselves into new creatures; we're dwelling in the cocoon. Our very posture says, I love you, God.

And sometimes, though not always, the moment rises inside us like a sound, and we can almost hear God's heart beating next to us.

Sitting While Jesus Prays

While attending a service at Grace Episcopal Church, I discovered another posture of waiting prayer. The Scripture reading that day recounted the last night of Jesus' life. One verse among the many caught my attention. I had heard it all my life but never really heard it at all. "And they went to a place which was called Gethsemane; and he said to his disciples, 'Sit here, while I pray'" (Mark 14:32).

It was the eve of Jesus' death. He was on the verge of being arrested. The hour was late, and the crisis surrounding the disciples had drained them inside and out. Jesus took them to a garden to wait through the long night. Did he ask them to pray? To plead his case? No. Sit down and rest, he said. I'll pray.

Sit here while I pray. I looked at the candles glowing in a quiet cluster on the altar and considered those words. Suddenly they became Christ's invitation not only to the disciples but to me. He wanted *me* to sit while he prayed.

What could this mean? I kept wondering. The notion was remote to me. Was the Spirit of Christ present and active within us, praying for us? Could it be that the prayer of waiting is being still and believing that Christ prays within us? I was thunderstruck by the idea.

I recalled a particular verse in the Bible, one that had always seemed cryptic to me. Back home after church I looked it up. "If we hope for what we do not see, we *wait* for it with patience. Likewise the Spirit helps us in our weakness; for we do not know how to pray as we ought, but the Spirit himself intercedes for us with sighs too deep for words" (Rom. 8: 25–26).

Dear God, I thought. You *do* pray in me while I wait. You pray with sighs too deep for words.

Spiritual writer Maggie Ross pursues this idea: "We delude ourselves that we pray: he only prays. Our act we call prayer is yielding to him and his prayer springing from the molten core of this love within us."[10]

To take upon ourselves the posture of sitting while Jesus prays brings us into the most grace-ful mystery of the waiting experience that there is: that of opening to the intimate presence of the Spirit praying within, penetrating, speaking, and holding us in our darkness.

Again the emphasis isn't on what we're doing but on what God is doing. Ultimately, we don't heal, transform, or create ourselves. We posture ourselves in ways that allow God to heal, transform, and create us. The posture of sitting while Jesus prays reminds us that the Spirit is active and speaking. Our part is to learn to sit, yielding to God's activity in us, opening ourselves to divine prayer, listening to the silent words. As Father Michael, a monk at the Abbey of Gethsemani, said to me, "Ultimately, waiting is letting God be God."

It's *rest* that characterizes this posture of waiting. To sit while Jesus prays is to take on a holy repose in which we relax the soul and find our rest in God. Rest in me, Christ seems to be saying. Rest in my prayer. And through our resting we're transformed.

Most of us have no idea how tired we are inside until we become still. As I thought about Jesus' invitation, I began to discover pockets of spiritual fatigue within me. Responding to crisis, pain, and questions of the soul takes lots of energy. Waiting needs to be a time of replenishing and storing spiritual energy. "Come to me, all who labor and are heavy laden, and I will give you rest," Jesus promises (Matt. 11:28).

Rest is just as holy as work. I like this story about Abbot Anthony, one of the desert fathers: A hunter came upon him and the brothers relaxing and resting in the wilderness and expressed his disapproval. Abbot Anthony told him to put an arrow in his bow and shoot it, which he did. Then the abbot had him shoot another—and another and another. The hunter protested that if he bent his bow all the time, it would break. "So it is also in the work of God. If we push ourselves beyond measure, the brethren will collapse. It is right, therefore, from time to time, to relax their efforts."[11]

In the drivenness of our society, it's hard to make time to relax our efforts and find transforming energy. That's why we need this particular posture of waiting so much. When we sit in this way we're relaxing the bow; we're coming to rest in a very deep way in God, allowing ourselves to be cradled in the sighing mystery of Christ's prayer.

When another desert father, Abbot Arsenius, asked God to lead him to salvation, a voice came to him, saying, "Be silent, rest in prayer." This is our call too.

The Greek word for *rest* is *hesychia*, a term that also came to mean *praying*. *Hesychasm* was a way of unceasing prayer in which a person descended into the heart and built a nest for herself and God, a place where she rested in the divine Presence, staying there throughout her day, throughout her pain, conflict, and struggle.

To sit while Jesus prays brings us to this kind of nesting in the heart. It allows us a replenishing rest in which we can be still and listen to the prayers and words that the Spirit whispers inside us. Julian of Norwich said that when a person is at ease or at rest with God, she "does not need to pray, but to contemplate reverently what God says."[12]

This happens best when we're still. Jesus knew that only in the stillness of our hearts could we relax on deep levels and become aware of the Voice in the hidden places of our soul, in the circumstances of our life, in the words and gestures around us, and in the beautiful face of creation.

I began to spend more of my time resting and opening myself to the prayer of Christ. I sat in a simplicity that holds us in being, and that posture opened space in me and generated new energies.

One day I told a friend who is a hospice volunteer about learning to sit while Jesus prays. "I have a story for you," she said. Then she told me about a woman named Maggie, who had fought valiantly for her life. Finally she grew weak and close to death. My friend said, "The first time I visited Maggie she asked me if I would pray. I told her that I wasn't much on praying out loud. She said that was all right; she would do it.

"Maggie prayed the most wonderful prayers. Toward the end, though, her strength ebbed and she got where she could barely talk, much less pray." My friend paused, and I saw a teardrop glisten in the lower lid of one eye. She wiped it away and went on: "One day Maggie whispered, 'I don't think I can pray today.' I told her I'd try, but Maggie shook her head. 'No, it's okay. We'll just sit here and let Jesus pray.' Maggie closed her eyes and rested on her pillow. Now and then she nodded her head as if she were listening, as if a Presence were speaking consoling words inside her. That's how we prayed until she died. We sat in her bedroom and let Jesus pray."

Many times in my experience of waiting I did not know how to pray or simply didn't have the strength for it. How wonderful it was to answer Jesus' invitation and sit while he prayed in me. I gave myself permission to rest. And in the stillness I listened, knowing that somewhere within me there really were sighs and whispers I could barely hear—the beautiful breath of God drawing me quietly toward new life, praying me slowly toward the light just as it had Maggie.

Sitting by the Road

In college I saw Samuel Beckett's play *Waiting for Godot*.[13] In it two tramps in baggy pants and bowler hats, Vladimir and Estragon, stand at the side of a country road day after day, waiting for the mysterious character of Godot to show up. Their wait forms the entire play.

No one seems to know who this Godot is—only that everything depends on his coming. If Godot comes "we'll be saved," goes a line at the end.

But slowly the truth sinks in. Godot isn't coming! Still the men go on waiting, in a strange, hopeless hope that at times is too unbearable to watch. Vladimir and Estragon, in their tramplike, almost clownish clothes, seem to be part of some sad cosmic joke.

As the play ends, they're still waiting. Godot hasn't come.

Some theater critics have suggested that Godot stands for God, or at least humanity's hope for Someone who would come and give everything meaning. It has also been suggested that Beckett wrote *Waiting for Godot* in reaction to Simone Weil's book *Waiting for God*, in which she put forth the idea that expectant waiting for God is the most important venture in life. Beckett seems to be portraying the nightmare of a hopeless wait, of waiting for a God who never shows.

I can still recall the rush of horror I felt as I left the theater. What if life is really like that, I thought. What if Vladimir and Estragon are really living the story of all of us?

Early in my crisis, as I struggled with the questions of midlife, that horror came back to me. Was I waiting for Godot? As the months of my waiting unfolded, I sometimes felt like Vladimir and Estragon at the side of the road, caught in futility, unable to see beyond the darkness, unable to trust that just over the next hill God was coming.

It can be so easy to lose hope in the midst of waiting. I realized that I needed a way of praying that could help me take on a posture of hoping and trusting. I tried to think of a biblical event that was more or less the opposite of waiting for Godot.

What I found was the story of Bartimaeus (Mark 10:46–52). Like Vladimir and Estragon, Bartimaeus waited along the side of a country road. He sat on a roadside outside Jericho, waiting for Jesus to come and heal his blindness. Also like the men in the play, Bartimaeus was something of a tramp—a "beggar", the Bible says. They shared blindness in common too. Bartimaeus was physically blind, while the men in Beckett's play were troubled by spiritual blindness.

With that, however, the similarities end. Unlike Vladimir and Estragon, Bartimaeus waited with hope and trust. He possessed an immense faith that God—healing, life, light, all of it—was coming soon, perhaps was just over the next hill. The other difference— and a rather supreme one at that—is that this time God showed up. I wanted to adopt the posture of Bartimaeus as part of my waiting prayer. *This* was the story that I wanted to live inside.

Can't you picture Bartimaeus sitting there, straining for the sound of footfalls along the road, hoping for a rising murmur among the crowd to signal Jesus' approach? We don't know how long he waited—only that when Jesus finally came by, Bartimaeus, filled with faith, asked for sight and received it. The gift of light— en*light*enment, de*light*, *light*ness—comes when we tap the places of hope and faith inside us.

When we adopt the posture of Bartimaeus, we sit still in our cocoon and uncover the places of hope and trust inside us. This can be hard to do when we're hanging upside down on God's tree and nothing in life looks the same anymore.

I might as well tell you, I fell into the story of Godot almost as much as the story of Bartimaeus. Without warning I would feel stuck, unable to believe that I could find my way through. My waiting would grow bleak, as if I were huddling on a frozen tundra where hope was the scarcest thing around. In his book *A Cry of Absence* Martin Marty uses the metaphor of the "white-out"—a blizzard that "can disorient, until a wanderer cannot know whether a dark object is a match cover nearby in the snow or a hut farther away on the horizon."[14] There are white-outs in waiting as well, times when, for whatever reason, hope vanishes and we're disoriented, unable to discern the shapes of God on the horizon, unable to trust that there's anything beyond our pain.

But we need to allow this disorientation. It's okay to doubt and to feel the remoteness of God sometimes. We all do it, if we're honest. And if we do nothing else in our waiting, we should be honest with ourselves. The white-outs pass more quickly and stay gone for longer periods in the face of honesty, and we come to a truer faith.

Paul Tournier reminds us that "he who has never doubted has never found true faith either."[15]

It helps, too, if we become still. We need to take on the posture of Bartimaeus as much as we're able, a little at a time. The prayer of waiting and stillness will eventually reorient us and ignite the warmth of hope.

One day, caught in a spiritual white-out, I sat still and tried to become Bartimaeus waiting on the road, to muster my faith that Christ was bringing me light even if I couldn't yet glimpse it. But I was having a hard time.

A voice within me said, like Bartimaeus, be a beggar. I hadn't considered that element of the story. What did being a beggar have to do with it? I didn't much like the suggestion, but I decided to at least reflect on it.

The first thing that popped into my head was that Jesus seemed to have a soft spot for the marginal people of life, including beggars. He healed, touched, and blessed them. He spoke highly of a beggar named Lazarus who lay under a rich man's table, begging for crumbs. I began to wonder why.

Could it be because beggars know how to open their hands, trusting that the crumbs of grace will fall? Is it because they have faith in something beyond themselves? Beggars are reduced by necessity to the sharp knowledge of their utter dependence. They have no bank accounts to fall back on, no investments or stocks or any of those things we think give us security and in which we place so much of our hope. A beggar must simply trust, moment by moment, that somehow she'll get fed. She lives off hope. She lives not with clenched fists but with palms open, ready to receive.

Nouwen wrote, "When you want to pray, then, the first question is: How do I open my closed hands?. . .Prayer is a way of life which allows you to find a stillness in the midst of the world where you open your hands to God's promises, and find hope for yourself."[16]

The beggar can teach us such prayer. She represents the part of us that's stripped to our essence, sitting ragged in our need with our hands wide open, trusting the holiness of life to hold us up.

This posture of dependency and trust can be glimpsed not only in Bartimaeus waiting on the road but in the Israelites waiting in the desert (Exod. 16). One of the best parts of their story comes when they realize that they have no food and nowhere to turn except toward God. "The desert is a symbol of two things: human extremity and God's self-giving," writes Alan Jones. "We need to be jolted out of our apparent self-sufficiency into the place of real need so God can give himself to us."[17]

It's the beggar who jolts us. In the desert the Israelites became beggars in the best sense of the word, opening their hands and trusting. And what happened? God sent manna. Not a forty-year supply to stockpile, but enough for one day. They had to hope and trust for tomorrow's, but it always came.

It made me think how true that principle of daily trust is in the experience of waiting. God sends us the strength and nourishment to heal, create, and become, *not* all at once but as we need it. Hope is the act of opening our palms day after day, trusting that we'll receive what we need.

Coming upon the drawing of homemade bread in my sketch pad one day, I copied Exodus 16:4 underneath it as a promise for the waiting heart to latch onto: "Behold, I will rain bread from heaven for you."

I began to try to find the beggar part of me. I sat in my stillness, in my blindness, in my beggar clothes. I touched my weakness, my humanity, my limitations. In touch with my neediness, I came face to face with my dependence on God—not only for my future but for my next breath. What can we do but acknowledge that dependence and trust God? In this posture of owning our weakness, we're transformed. For that's how the soul is born and reborn: as we quit servicing the ego and acknowledge our weakness. Strength in weakness is the paradox of the cocoon.

A whole new poetry of strength and hope began to be written in me. Sometimes in my stillness I heard myself repeating, God comes. Light is stronger than darkness; God comes. Bread rains from heaven; God comes.

Slowly my hands opened to catch the crumbs.

"For what do I wait?" asked the psalmist. "My hope is in thee" (Ps. 39:7). When we sit at the side of the road like Bartimaeus, those words become the drama playing out inside our heart.

TOGETHER IN STILLNESS

One afternoon as the children watched television and I folded laundry, we heard a terrible thud against the patio door. I turned in time to see blue wings falling to the ground. A bird had flown into the glass.

None of us said a word. We looked at one another and crept to the door. The children followed me outside. I half-expected the bird to be dead, but she wasn't. She was stunned and her right wing was a little lopsided, but it didn't look broken—bruised, maybe.

The bird sat perfectly still, her eyes tiny and afraid. She looked so fragile and alone that I sat down beside her. I reached out my little finger and brushed her wing.

A voice came from behind me. "Why doesn't it fly off, Mama?"

"She's hurt," I said. "She just needs to be still."

We watched her. We watched her stillness. Finally the children wandered back to the television, satisfied that nothing was going to "happen" for a while. But I couldn't leave her.

I sat beside her, unable to resist the feeling that we shared something, the two of us. The wounds and brokenness of life. Crumpled wings. A collision with something harsh and real. I felt like crying for her. For myself. For every broken thing in the world.

That moment taught me that while the postures of stillness within the cocoon are frequently an individual experience, we also need to share our stillness. The bird taught me anew that we're all in this together, that we need to sit in one another's stillness and take up corporate postures of prayer. How wonderful it is when we can be honest and free enough to say to one another, "I need you to wait with me," or, "Would you like me to wait with you?"

I studied the bird, deeply impressed that she seemed to know instinctively that in stillness is healing. I had been learning that too, learning that stillness can be the prayer that transforms us. How much more concentrated our stillness becomes, though, when it's shared.

The door opened again. "Is she finished being still yet?" Ann asked.

"No, not yet," I said, knowing that I was talking as much about myself as the bird. We went on waiting together. Twenty minutes. Thirty. Fifty.

Finally she was finished being still. She cocked her head to one side, lifted her wings, and flew. The sight of her flying made me catch my breath. From the corner of my eye I saw her shadow move along the ground and cross over me. Grace is everywhere, I thought. Then I picked myself up and went back to folding laundry.

After that day, when I needed someone to pray with me I called on one of my friends and simply asked if she would come and wait with me. Sometimes we sat together without saying a word. Even then, however, our hearts were focused and attentive and beating with love. We were listening as best we could to the prayer the Spirit prays within us. We were trusting together, hoping in high shadows and the flight of wings.

I have regrets in life, but waiting with that wounded bird isn't one of them. I learned her stillness and her flight. She taught me prayer.

Chapter 7

Incubating the Darkness

I said to my soul, be still, and let the dark come upon you
Which shall be the darkness of God.

T. S. ELIOT

Lord,
      I will tear the heart of my soul in two
      And you must lay therein.
      You must lay yourself
      In the wounds of my soul.

MECHTILD OF MAGDEBURG

The week before Easter I began to sink into an inscrutable inner darkness unlike any I had ever experienced. A spiritual night. What was it? An emptying, a stripping away? A collapsing of the old order? Had I reached the bottom?

I felt that I had been dropped into an abyss of unknowing, into a stark confrontation with my own pain and wounds. The darkness seemed to encircle me on every side. At times I felt abandoned and afraid inside its roundness. At other times the darkness felt strangely nurturing, swollen with the mystery of becoming. I wondered if this was what one encountered at the heart of the chrysalis.

Baffled and wrenched by the blackness of the passage I was in, I sat on my bed, cradled my journal in my lap, and poured out my thoughts and feelings:

145

Palm Sunday. I feel as if a candle has blown out inside me. Earlier today I read a passage from *New Seeds of Contemplation* in which Merton said that if the person who has come upon the spiritual dark night is carried away with impatience, "he will run away from the darkness, and do the best he can to dope himself with the first light that comes along."[1] That's my temptation. This idea of remaining in the darkness is foreign to me. I'm a light-seeking creature and an impatient one at that. But could it be that seeking light, real light, not the artificial stuff, comes only by dwelling for a time in the dark? (Dear Lord, I don't think I can stand one more paradox!)

Merton also wrote these encouraging words:

> When they stay quiet in the muteness of naked truth, resting in a simple and open-eyed awareness, attentive to the darkness which baffles them, a subtle and indefinable peace begins to seep into their souls and occupies them with a deep and inexplicable satisfaction.... What is it? It is hard to say: but one feels that it is somehow summed up in "the will of God" or simply, "God."[2]

Summed up in *God*? For me the darkness is partially summed up in the word *Question*. I feel wrapped in an awful, silent pondering that doesn't know any answers, only questions. It makes me think of that odd moment when, as a child, I kicked a ball into the air and it never came down. (I didn't see it wedged between two branches of a pine tree.) I stood on the grass, mystified, waiting. I felt then as I feel now. As if my life were up in the air. I keep waiting for the answers to fall out of the sky, but they don't. There should be more gravity in waiting, more logic, it seems.

The darkness gets excruciating. In fact, the other word that sums up my darkness is *tension*. In this dark cave of my own being, I'm brought into sharper contact with my pain. At night shadows that I can't see in daylight play on the wall. I see my wounds, my conflicts, my incompleteness, and my longing in heightened outlines on the walls of my soul.

I'd like to be rid of this darkness. To unwrap the cocoon. Get busy. Do something to take my mind off my "suffering," latch onto some easy, neon answer that will camouflage the shadows. But I have the sense lurking inside that there's a mystery unfolding in the darkness that can't come any other way.

Could it be that this is a holy dark?

I closed my journal, then wrapped my arms around my knees and let the tears flow quietly from my eyes. They ran in tiny rivulets down my bare legs. I watched them, sensing that they were the birth waters in which I would become new.

THE DARKNESS OF THE WOMB

A couple of days after writing the Palm Sunday passage in my journal, I dragged out the little wooden tree that we decorated with Easter eggs every year. It was a family tradition that Ann and I would pierce the eggshells at each end with a needle, blow out the insides, then paint the exteriors and hang the empty eggs on the tree.

As we emptied out the eggs that year, Ann looked at the collected contents and asked, "Is this what makes a baby chicken?"

"If the eggs had been allowed to incubate long enough, chicks would have formed out of this," I told her.

A pensive look came over her face. "I kind of wish they could have become chickens instead of Easter eggs," she said.

I went on working, but a little more reflectively. My daughter's words caused me to think how sad it really is when we don't incubate the new life pressing to birth inside us. How sad when we cut it short, forcing unformed answers and refusing to hold the tensions of pain. How sad when we become empty, painted shells hanging on God's tree.

Thomas Keating, a Trappist monk and writer, expresses our calling: "The greatest accomplishment in life is to be what we are, which is God's idea of what He wanted us to be when He brought us into being. . . . Accepting that gift is accepting God's will for us, and in its acceptance is found the path to growth and ultimate fulfillment."[3]

Every time I passed the completed egg tree that week, I thought about the process of incubation, of fulfilling "God's idea." To *incubate* means to create the conditions necessary for development. What were those conditions, I wondered. Then it hit me: *darkness*. Everything incubates in darkness. And I knew that the darkness in which I found myself *was* a holy dark. I was incubating something new.

Whenever new life grows and emerges, darkness is crucial to the process. Whether it's the caterpillar in the chrysalis, the seed in the ground, the child in the womb, or the True Self in the soul, there's always a time of waiting in the dark.

One of the more interesting conversations recorded in the Bible took place between Jesus and a high-ranking Pharisee named Nicodemus (John 3:1–8). Jesus told him that in order to see the kingdom of God, a person had to be born again. When Nicodemus wanted to know how a person could enter his mother's womb a second time, Jesus made it clear that he was talking about a *spiritual* birth, one that takes place inside us.

As Christians we've always emphasized the spiritual birth, but we haven't paid a lot of attention to the incubation that precedes it—all those months in the darkness of the womb. When Jesus selected this beautiful feminine metaphor, he wanted us to grasp the importance not only of new birth but of *how* that birth happens. I think he was implying that with every birth there is a womb, and if we want to find the inner kingdom, we will have to enter the place of waiting, darkness, and incubation.

In that remarkable conversation Jesus was telling us how to grow and become. Spiritual life is an ongoing experience of spiritual gestation, of giving birth to deeper dimensions of wholeness. We enter the spiritual womb many times. As the Bible says, "We...are being changed into his likeness from one degree of glory to another" (2 Cor. 3:18), in other words, birth by birth.

"If we are to be soul makers, we must not reject the idea of the womb," wrote my friend and author Djohariah Toor. "In the spiritual world, authentic life is born out of silence and waiting."[4] But entering the darkness isn't easy. Fear of that step is a common spiritual phobia. We fear the shadows on our own wall. We're terrified of encountering things that go bump in the night of our soul.

When I was pregnant with my daughter, my son Bob was three years old and scared of the dark. We put a nightlight in his room, but sometimes he still cried out for me in the middle of the night.

One night as I held him against me to comfort him, he touched my rounded abdomen and asked, "Mama, is it dark inside there where my little brother is?" (He was convinced that his sister was a boy.)

"Yes," I said, "it's dark in there.

"He doesn't even have a nightlight, does he?"

"No, not even a nightlight," I said.

Bob patted my abdomen. I patted him. Finally he asked, "Do you think my brother is scared all by himself in there?"

"I don't think so, because he's not really alone. He's inside of me." Suddenly I had an inspiration. I said, "And it's the same way with you. When it's dark and you think you're all by yourself, you really aren't. I carry you inside me too. Right here in my heart."

I looked into his face, wondering if he understood what I meant. He didn't say anything; he simply lay back down and went to sleep. That was the last time he called out in fear of the night.

When we enter the spiritual night, we can feel alone, encompassed by a fearful darkness. What we need to remember is that we're carried in God's womb, in God's divine heart, even when we don't know it, even when God seems far away. That's been my growing awareness. First God was only "up there." Then God was "all around." Next I began to see that God was also "within me." And now, most shocking of all, I was finding that I am and always was "within God."

"TIP ME OVER AND POUR ME OUT"

One day, while I was praying in stillness, the lines of a song I had sung during a tap-dance recital when I was five meandered into my head. I had been dressed up as a teapot. (That's right, a teapot.) The song went as follows:

> I'm a little teapot, short and stout.
> Here is the handle; here is the spout.
> If you turn the heat up, I will shout,
> "Tip me over and pour me out!"

I interrupted my prayer with laughter. But as I meditated on the song, it occurred to me that the dance of the teapot is the dance we all do in the dark night.

We're containers filled with an ego elixir we've brewed ourselves. When the heat is turned up inside and the old begins to burn away, we must offer God the handle and the spout of our lives. God tips us over and pours us out. The "me" is poured out: the self with a lowercase *s*, the old ways of being, the old ways of relating to God. We're emptied so that we can be refilled with new and living waters.

Midlife is a time of tipping over. It is a good time to learn that simple little song. It gave me a way of thinking about my experience that wasn't mysterious and threatening. I was dancing a childhood dance, that's all. And if I ever got to feeling terribly "spiritual" about it all, I imagined myself in that ridiculous teapot costume and that took care of that.

"Tip me over and pour me out" is the underlying theme of the spiritual dark. Written about for centuries in the classics of spiritual literature, that process is accepted as a necessary and universal passage in spiritual transformation. It's often referred to as the "dark night of the soul" or the "dazzling darkness."

"There comes a time when both body and soul enter into such a vast darkness that one loses light," wrote Mechtild of Magdeburg. There comes a time when the soul "sinks down into the night."[5]

John of the Cross, who wrote volumes about this experience, explained that a person may suffer a feeling of abandonment by God, as well as dryness, emptiness, and a distressing encounter with her own hunger.

We don't hear much about the "dark night" anymore. The one and only sermon I ever heard preached on darkness was riveting, however. The minister pointed out that the most significant events in Jesus' life took place in darkness: his birth, his arrest, his death, his resurrection. His point was that although darkness in the spiritual life has gotten a lot of bad press, it sometimes yields extraordinary events.

What extraordinary event is taking place in the dark night of the soul? We're receiving a loving call from God to move into a wider and deeper dimension of the spiritual life. We're being *emptied* of the old. It becomes *darkened* to us. As John of the Cross wrote, the purpose of the dark night is to purge us.[6]

Previous ways of thinking about and relating to God no longer suffice. Old religious acts no longer bring the consolation they once did. Former patterns and selves feel like outgrown sweaters.

Merton tells us that the darkness comes when we allow God to strip away the false selves and make us into the persons we're meant to be.[7] Transformation depends on this stripping away (or "denuding," as John of the Cross called it), a process that involves undoing ego patterns, recasting the old story we created for ourselves to live in, and unraveling illusions not only about ourselves but about God.

This stripping away both demands and creates a temporary darkness. It's almost as if the burning up of old patterns and the accompanying illumination that comes from discovering the True Self create a light so bright that it blinds us for a while.

In the ensuing darkness God often seems absent. We begin to encounter *Deus absconditis*—the sense that God is playing hide and seek. I believe that what we're experiencing, however, is the hiding of an old way of knowing and experiencing God, the crumbling of our "creation" of who God is and the divine system that our egos have invested in.

After a midlife workshop I conducted for a group of Lutheran women in Illinois, one woman described her dark night to me. "It's as if God lifted the lid of a music box in a dark room inside of me and then vanished. It's a beautiful tune, a new sound; and hearing it, I can't forget it. I'm like a child leaving my nursery, stumbling through a dark house in search of the Music Maker. But often I have no idea where to turn. I only know I can't go back."

In the darkness God becomes the Ungraspable Mystery, the one who unleashes a tune so spellbinding that we're compelled to follow, to stumble through shadowed corridors until we find the source of it. We're being drawn beyond where we are into an entirely new way of relating to God, one that's beyond anything we've even imagined.

When we give ourselves to spiritual journeying, we soon realize that God always invites us beyond where we are. A friend who backpacks the Carolina mountains expressed this truth with humor: "If you sign up for God's hike, don't bother to pack the tent. Just when you think you're ready to make camp, God will wave you on to some new site."

God guides us the long way round. And sometimes that means winding through a dark wood. It doesn't mean we're lost, however. The darkness is part of the trip. Too many of us panic in the dark. We don't understood that it's a *holy* dark and that the idea is to surrender to it and journey through to real light.

NIGHT TRAVELERS

In the last few years, to my surprise, a number of people sought me out to talk about their spiritual journeys. Many of them were upset and confused; invariably they told me how "dark" things were. Like me, they were traveling the spiritual night.

While each was unique, together they formed a composite profile: They were reeling from a crisis and in pain. They were anguished by the contradiction of who they were and who they hoped to be. They were facing the illusions and pretenses they had lived by. They were being introduced to their counterfeit selves and recognizing their lifelong and futile attempts to be someone other than who they truly were.

"Life isn't what I thought," they frequently told me. "It's not supposed to be like this!" (We're always aghast when life doesn't live up to our expectations and ideals.)

I once saw a Gary Larson cartoon in which wagon trains were under siege by the Indians. A couple of arrows with fire on the end hit the wagons, and they began to burn. One cowboy turned to another and said, "Hey! They're lighting their arrows! Can they *do* that?"

I chuckled, but my heart went out to that cowboy. He was experiencing the stab of stunned injustice that we all get when life delivers a fiery arrow and the "world" we've spent our lives creating and believing in starts to burn. We want to scream, "Hey! Can life *do* this? It's not supposed to be like this!"

If we can get past the shocked denial, we're able to enter the dark and be reborn. We can begin to wrestle with the dark angels in our lives. We can give ourselves permission to ask questions: What newness does God beckon me toward? What do I do when things are "upside down"? What are the patterns that need to be shed so that my True Self can emerge? What are the wounds that need to be healed? What "lost coin" in me needs to be found? What "lost sheep" in me needs to be shepherded?

I found that, like me, the night travelers I spoke with were not only appalled by the darkness but outraged that old answers no longer worked. Some, having little idea that they were in a profound tunnel of transformation, wanted to know how to dispel the darkness and get back to the familiar sunshine again.

Because our stories are the best "bread" we can offer one another, I tried to tell the travelers about my own tracks through the dark. I also suggested that it seems to me we can't really go back to the *old* sunshine; instead, we're being drawn to a new Light. I asked them to listen to the Voice in their soul and try to discern whether their darkness was an invitation from God. I asked them to consider whether they were being asked to incubate more of their True Self. Most of all, I tried to remind them of who they really were. Then I hugged them, knowing that their night was my night and my night was theirs.

EASTERING

Thoughts of incubation and the spiritual womb lingered with me all through Holy Week. At sunset the day before Easter I went to Grace Episcopal Church for the Holy Saturday service. The sanctuary was dark except for a trace of sunlight filtering through the stained-glass window at the back. I knelt in the pew, as is the custom. I had come to remember Jesus in his tomb, in his darkness, in his waiting. I wanted to wait with him the same way I'd waited with the wounded bird in my backyard.

I suppose I'd also come looking for some way to wait in my own darkness, to turn it into the kind of dark night that could incubate newness. Darkness remains deadening and nontransforming—like the tomb—unless we learn how to turn it into a creative and life-giving experience.

· As I knelt there, the wounds and broken places in my past, the conflict in my present and the questions surrounding my future became an awful throb in my chest. I felt the tensions pull until there was a small crescendo of pain inside me. The darkness closed in.

I moved from my knees back onto the seat. My thoughts about Jesus waiting in the tomb for Easter began to blend with the thoughts I'd had during the week about the soul waiting in the womb for new birth. *Womb* and *tomb*. The two words resonated in me. As I listened to the rhyme of sound and then to the rhyme of meaning, I heard the words with new clarity. The darkness of Jesus' tomb became a place of transformation, a womb, the waiting room of new life. The darkness of death was transformed into a life-giving dark.

Can this happen within *us* as well? I believe so. Julian of Norwich wrote that our *wounds* become the *womb*. This touching image points us to the awareness that transformation hinges on our ability to turn our pain (the tomb) into a fertile place where life is birthed (the womb).

There in the church, the question filled me: How could I transform the darkness of Holy Saturday into the darkness of the womb?

We had reached the point in the service when the Paschal candle is lit as a reminder that in spite of the darkness of Jesus' tomb, the radiance of new life is coming. "The light of Christ," the priest said as he held the fire to the candle. The little flame caught and flickered in the darkness, disappeared, then returned, quivering on and off in a draft of wind. I thought of the line I'd written in my journal earlier in the week. "I feel as if a candle has blown out inside me." The strange synchronicity made my heart beat faster.

I didn't want that candle to go out. Suddenly the priest lifted his hands and cupped them around the flame. As the light of the candle grew stronger, the sight of him cradling that little speck of fire burned into me. It was an image of bare, unscripted grace: the light of Christ.

Throughout the service I gazed at the candle's flame. I thought of a man I'd once interviewed in Columbia, South Carolina, who had been blind from birth. Late in life he underwent an operation that restored his sight. When the bandages were removed, the first thing he saw—the first thing he saw in his whole life—was a tiny tear-shaped drop glistening on the end of an eyedropper. He told me, "That drop was the most awesome, beautiful thing. It filled me with love." That was how I felt about the little tear-shaped drop of light glistening on the candle. I looked at it as if I'd never seen its like before. It was the most awesome, beautiful thing; it filled me with love.

When I left the church, I carried that tiny piece of Easter fire inside me. This fire, which belongs to us all, is nothing less than the pulse of new life within the soul. That Holy Saturday I heard God say to me, Cup your hands around it.

There's a line from a poem by Gerard Manley Hopkins that speaks to me: "Let him easter in us, be a dayspring to the dimness of us, be a crimson-cresseted east."[8] Until I read that line it had never occurred to me to think of *Easter* as a verb. But it is, isn't it? Easter isn't only a long-ago event that happened but an *action* that goes on happening inside us today.

To "let him easter in us" is to let the Christ-life incubate within the darkness of our waiting. The Christ-life is like the Paschal candle sputtering in the darkness. We need gentle hands cupped around it, coaxing the flame to grow stronger.

I learned that in transformation we mustn't run from the darkness but must rather coax the Easter light inside it. I learned that we turn the darkness of the tomb into the darkness of the womb by cupping our hands around the pulse of True Life and helping it grow.

LIVE THE QUESTIONS

One way we coax the life of the new self is by living the questions that inhabit our dark night, by dwelling creatively with the unresolved inside us.

I lived with questions about who I had been and who I was becoming, and about whether the growth was worth the pain, risk, and upheaval. I lived with questions about how to adopt parts of myself that I had orphaned, how to heal old wounds, how to relate to an expanding vision of God and the world.

I didn't like the disorder and anxiety the questions produced, and I didn't like the unknowing. At the height of all this I came upon a little book by the poet Rainer Maria Rilke. It altered the way I felt about the questions. Here's part of what I read:

> I beg you. . .to be patient toward all that is unsolved in your heart and to try to love the *questions themselves* like locked rooms and like books that are written in a very foreign tongue. Do not now seek the answers, which cannot be given you because you would not be able to live them. And the point is, to live everything. *Live* the questions now. Perhaps you will then gradually, without noticing it, live along some distant day into the answer.[9]

Okay, I told myself, embrace the questions, *live* them. That's a difficult order. We're trained to *answer* questions, and if we can't answer them, to ignore them. I once saw a poster on a wall with these words, attributed to the eminent family therapist Virginia Satir: "Most people prefer the certainty of misery to the misery of uncertainty."[10] That's worth pondering.

Living with questions can indeed be a miserable experience. We like things fixed, figured out, and nailed down, even if that means being nailed to a false and static existence. Questions terrify us, because they're like hammers prying up the nails.

People who want life hammered down into tight, legalistic certainties seem to me to be the people most insecure inside. Frankly, the folks who frighten me the most are those who are dead certain about everything, who have all the answers and no questions.

Have we Christians forgotten the transforming value of a question? When we extinguish questions from our lives, there's little if any developing consciousness. We block ourselves from new truths and possibilities.

Kierkegaard distinguished between Christendom and Christianity: he said that the former is what we've made of the latter. Like our fear of the dark, the fear of questions in the spiritual life belongs to Christendom, not Christianity.

The most exciting people in my life are those who punctuate life with questions as frequently as periods. When I ask my mentor, Beatrice, a question, she sometimes responds not with an answer but with an even bigger question. Sometimes my soul has to get on tiptoe just to hear it.

Beatrice wrote of the importance of going into our heart, our inmost self, and turning attention to such "Great Questions" as, "What is this life of ours all about? Why are we here? What kind of being are we?...What is it in me that knows? and knows that it knows that it knows? What is my deepest nature?...*Really asking* such questions is praying."[11]

Jesus was a master at using questions to pull people into self-confrontation and growth. "What are you looking for?" "Do you want to get well?" "Who do you say that I am?" "Why do you not understand what I say?" "Do you love me?" The New Testament is full of them.

My friend Betty and I meet regularly to ponder questions. We ask such things as, What would it mean for us to really love? How am I experiencing God at this moment in my life? What darkness in me needs to be confronted and transformed? A fellow questioner helps us learn how to *live* our questions instead of suppressing them.

There's an art to living your questions. You peel them. You listen to them. You let them spawn new questions. You hold the unknowing inside. You linger with it instead of rushing into half-baked answers. Jesuit priest and writer Anthony de Mello puts it well: "Some people will never learn anything because they grasp too soon. Wisdom, after all, is not a station you arrive at, but a manner of traveling. . . . To know exactly where you're headed may be the best way to go astray. Not all who loiter are lost."[12]

As a matter of fact, those who "loiter" in the question long enough will "live into" the answer. "Seek and ye shall find," said Jesus (Matt. 7:7). I sometimes read that as, "Seek *long enough* and ye shall find." You see, it's the patient act of dwelling in the darkness of a question that eventually unravels the answer.

Christianity (not necessarily Christendom) has also recognized that when we shovel through the dark layers of self with our questions, we discover not only knowledge of self but knowledge of God. The anonymous author of *The Cloud of Unknowing* advises that you seek "to obtain for yourself a true knowledge and feeling of yourself as you are; and then I believe that soon afterward you will have a true knowledge and feeling of God as He is."[13]

As the weeks of spring melted into summer, I struggled to live inside my questions. In some manner they produced a vibration in my soul that made it malleable. The tension of the question itself seemed to bend and reshape me, drawing awareness into my path.

Jacob Needleman quotes a Christian monk named Father Sylvan as saying that questions teach *by themselves*. Now *there's* a revolutionary idea. Father Sylvan believed that the growth of a person's soul was "activated" whenever she experienced the pain of contradiction or the sustained state of questioning. In other words, the actual groping and searching is the way our deeper self evolves and is released. "Always seek the Question," he wrote. "It is through the medium of total self-inquiry that the forces of good and evil can meet and be reconciled within us."[14]

When I was so deep in that dark that I couldn't see a way out, "knowing" happened gradually, slowly, as I lived the questions without forcing anything. A God-given enlightenment dawned from inside out. It welled up out of the sacred fermenting that was taking place within me.

There are some things that we must simply wait to receive. We live our questions and wait for the knowing to happen. Like the tree, we wait for the sap to rise.

HOLD THE TENSIONS

Another way in which we can transform our darkness and "easter" the life of the new self is by holding the painful tensions within us—the tugs between what the ego wants and that to which the True Self calls us.

We're filled with an array of opposing tensions. John of the Cross wrote that in the dark night "the soul becomes a battlefield in which...two contraries combat one another."[15] We're pulled between the opposites: good and evil, hope and despair, love and hate, forgiveness and revenge, venturing forth and staying put, the urge to wholeness and the pull to fragmentation, acceptance and rejection, commitment and freedom, community and solitude, intimacy and autonomy, *psyche* and *soma*, doing and being, consciousness and unconsciousness, the masculine and the feminine. The list goes on and on.

Living with such conflicting dualities has torn the curtain of our interior life. Many of us are shredded inside, split, unable to grow beyond our fragmentation and woundedness.

The first step toward growth is to enter these tensions, embracing and exploring the pain and ambiguity within rather than running from them, concealing them, or anesthetizing them.

Few choose this path, however. We're more apt to try to quell the conflict by banishing the unwanted side of the opposites. For instance, we may deny and repress our evil intentions and motivations while remaining conscious of our good side, thereby locking our darker side in the mind's cellar—in what Jung called the "unconscious shadow." The shadow side doesn't disappear, of course. It grows in the dark and plays havoc with our lives.

In the same way, we may allow the nurturing-mother side of ourselves and banish the part of us that desires to venture into the world with a career. Or perhaps we allow the career woman free rein and banish the mother. We may allow the Little Red Hen and repress the playful child inside us. We may allow Rapunzel and repress our autonomous self. We may allow Chicken Little and reject our daring self. We may allow the Tin Woodman and reject our sexual self. We may allow the achiever and abandon the side of us that wants a vocation of simply being. We may allow the unblemished side of us and disregard the part that's wounded.

Before long we have an entire hidden orphanage inside us—a group of lost and alienated parts of the self that we've banished. Lost sisters, unlived lives. At midlife these orphans cry out to be heard. As the voices rise, so does the tension.

God calls us to the unifying and healing of our soul. God is *beyond* opposites. In God, everything is whole, is one. What's more, God made us for oneness, to know wholeness and harmony. God desires that we reconcile these opposing forces within us, that we "come together" inside and be more unified in our consciousness—with a "single eye" as Jesus said (Matt. 6:22 KJV).

This interior integration and healing of the soul is our aim. But it can't happen if we avoid the pain and tensions within us. Once, when my counselor and I were discussing Joseph Campbell's captivating dictum "Follow your bliss,"[16] he commented, "It may be just as important to follow your agony." Perhaps we can't find our real bliss until we begin to confront our agony.

The poet Gibran wrote something similar: "Your joy is your sorrow unmasked. The self-same well from which your laughter rises was oftentimes filled with your tears....The deeper that sorrow carves into your being, the more joy you can contain." [17]

When we enter the darkness, we accept that there will be trials. In the clash of opposites, the pain and conflict pull the strands of our lives back and forth in a miserable tug of war. This wrestling, which Merton called *"agonia,"* is seen vividly in Paul's exclamation, "I do not understand my own actions. For I do not do what I want, but I do the very thing I hate" (Rom. 7:15). He was strung between the opposites inside himself.

I grew familiar with that situation myself. Circumstances often arose in which opposing internal factions came into tension. One summer day, when I had been sitting at my desk for three hours without a break, a voice in me said, Get up, go outside, and feel the grass under your feet and the sun on your nose. *Be* for a while. You have all the time you need. You're eternal.

A second voice, which I recognized as the blended voice of my Tinsel Star and the Little Red Hen, said, Stay where you are. Work. Strive. Do. You have deadlines. You do *not* have all the time you need. You've got to scramble to get anywhere. Life is all about working hard so that you can get ahead and shine brightly.

Intellectually, I knew which was the best voice for me to obey, but I felt "captured" by the "ego logic" of the Star and Little Red Hen. A small example, perhaps, but there I was, hung between the opposites.

I had been maintaining a heavy speaking schedule, and the number of engagements was wearing on me. Why are you compelled to do so many? I asked myself. Why not cut them in half? Part of me wanted balance, wanted to cut back. The other part said, If you cut back, you'll diminish your career. You won't shine as brightly. Everybody knows you have to "promote" yourself if you want to get ahead.

What a nasty, embarrassing little voice that latter one was! I asked myself why in the world I thought I needed to "promote" myself. What caused me to feel that way? Could I risk giving up "success"? The tensions went to the heart of my Tinsel Star, and they were painful. Yet I sensed that by engaging them, a new, more genuine self could be released. (In the end I cut my speaking in half.)

I probably suffered most from the powerful tensions created by my Little Girl with a Curl. Deep inside she was afraid of being abandoned and unloved. Her insecurity could be shattering as well as driving.

The tension to please, to be the "best little girl in the world," to live up to everyone's ideals so that I would have their approval, clashed continually with the growing tug in me to respond out of my *real* self—out of love not fear, out of honesty rather than approval seeking.

Holding such tensions meant asking myself in countless circumstances, Am I being true in this moment, or am I forfeiting truth in order to please the person in front of me and gain acceptance? Am I responding out of fear?

A forty-year-old friend told me, "I've lived my whole life to please my parents. I never really explored my own thoughts and dreams; rather, I sought my parents' acceptance by becoming a carbon copy of them. Now I want to be an original, but it seems a fearsome thing to risk."

HEALING THE WOUNDS

The next step in the growth process is to learn to hold the tensions creatively, in such a way that they draw us toward healing. John Shea writes, "This experience of internal war pushes us beyond ourselves. We become aware of the Mystery we dwell within and look to it for explanation and healing."[18] Pushed out of ourselves, we leave space for Mystery, for the healing alchemy of God.

"How long must I bear pain in my soul?" wrote the psalmist (13:2). Long enough—that's the answer.

I recall mixing two chemical substances in a crucible and placing them over a Bunsen burner back in my college chemistry lab. The substances came together and simmered as my partner and I waited for a threshold level to be achieved. Finally the substance changed color and became a brand-new compound.

A similar spiritual alchemy can go on inside us. When we enter the crucible of darkness and bring the painful tensions of our lives together to simmer creatively, a threshold level is eventually reached in which healing, "knowing," strength—a new synthesis of being—takes place. Our waiting changes color and turns golden.

That summer I walked by Ann's room and saw her brown-haired porcelain doll tipped over on the shelf. As I righted it, I noticed a wisp of hair dangling across the doll's face. Little Girl with a Curl, I thought.

At once I felt a rush of pain. I thought of the little girl in me who had been wounded enough by life that she took on the pattern of pleasing and adapting to the expectations around her, so fearful of disapproval and of straying outside the lines that she often gave her uniqueness away.

I sank into Ann's rocking chair, determined to hold the tensions of pain. After a while, through a blur of tears, I noticed that I was rocking the doll. I managed a smile, for I realized that I was rocking and embracing what symbolized a wounded part of me. I was holding her close and loving her.

Every false self has a wound inside that needs to be healed. In those moments I felt the movements of healing inside, as if the tensions had given way to something new. Ritualizing my healing had opened a way for God to release a transformative power that touched the wounded place. That completely spontaneous event had helped to "oneth my soul," as Julian of Norwich put it.

To suffer our darkness is to take the pained and broken parts of ourselves and rock them gently. We enter the rhythm of our own aching lives. In so doing, we offer the wounded parts of us love and forgiveness, and we accept *God's* love and forgiveness. Back and forth we rock the tensions, until the transcendent begins to break through and God infuses us with the new.

Rilke said that the person who suffers needs to stay with it, must not be a "waster of sorrows." He noted elsewhere that "the more still, more patient and more open we are when we are sad, so much the deeper and so much the more unswervingly does the new go into us, so much the better do we make it ours, so much the more will it be our destiny."[19]

Healing the Tin Woodman part of me—the part that had split her body and her soul, her heart and her head—has been long and difficult. I began by creating a kind of dialogue with my heart. I often paused and asked myself what I was feeling at a particular moment. *Really* feeling. I tried to listen deeply. I was often amazed at the internal silence I encountered. Sometimes my feelings seemed locked up, numbed, indistinguishable. Gradually, though, as I continued with the dialogue and gave myself permission to have real feelings—and not only that, to "feel" them and even respond out of that authentic feeling—I began to be reconnected to my heart in new ways.

Likewise, learning to descend into the body and create a loving and accepting relationship with it is a vital work of spiritual wholeness for a woman. As I mention in Chapter Three, I had not been very present to my body in the years prior to this spiritual journey. My attitude toward it had been one of apathy and tolerance. I had never been able to truly welcome my physical side; I lived mostly in my head. Even while jogging or exercising, I usually became lost in my ideas and thoughts. Now I worked at setting up a creative dialogue with my body as I had with my heart. I listened to it. I tried to be aware of it, to give it love and gentle touches, to "feel" and "know" myself inside it (to *be* a body, not just have one). I began to consciously acknowledge the wonderful, sensual music God had placed in me and to bless it, to recognize my body as a receptacle of holiness.

Some days, when I was all alone in the house, I danced, letting my body express itself, reverencing its movements, delighting in its energies, and being present to its rhythms. I was freeing it to be. The Bible says, after all, that there's a "time to dance" (Eccles. 3:4). My dancing became a kind of contemplative movement, a prayer that began to help integrate me, to knit my body back to my soul.

Slowly I experienced a new "communion" with my lost heart and my lost body. One day I enacted the communion. I took the tiny Communion cup I'd brought back from Jerusalem when I'd traveled there several years ago. I filled it with juice, and took a scrap of bread. Then I drank and ate. It was a symbolic act of sharing the cup and breaking bread with those lost parts of me and accepting them back into my fellowship. I'll never forget how powerful that moment was for me. Holiness and a sense of homecoming washed over me as I celebrated the healing of the split, the presence of Christ that binds back what is torn.

When we begin to rock the tensions creatively back and forth, refusing to "waste our sorrows," daring to ritualize both our pain and our healing, we move to the critical threshold where our waiting changes color and transformation begins.

TAKING UP YOUR CROSS

Holding your tensions can be compared to the biblical idea of taking up your cross. We allow ourselves inwardly to become stretched between two poles moving in opposite directions. Nailed to the opposites, we hang between the tensions, among the wounds. And we remain there out of love.

Catherine of Siena wrote, "Nails were not enough to hold God-and-man nailed and fastened on the cross, had not love kept him there."[20] Out of love we take up the tensions of our darkness voluntarily, for the sole purpose of emerging to a more genuine life in which God's image is enlivened within us. We endure it in order to find what is real in us and break through to life. This is what it means to suffer creatively; it's the suffering that "easters" us.

Creative suffering can be contrasted with neurotic suffering, in which a person takes on a self-pitying style of living because she gets sympathy or control or security from it. Neurotic suffering is untransforming and isn't undertaken for the reason of becoming more whole. It doesn't end in resurrection but in despair and alienation. As author Marion Woodman expressed it, "Real suffering burns clean; neurotic suffering creates more and more soot."[21]

Creative suffering is the pain we encounter in confronting our lives honestly, expanding our vision, choosing a new way, owning our shadow, and healing wounds.

Some of my midlife suffering came from holding the tensions within my marriage. While Sandy and I were away for a weekend at a lakeside cabin, the internal wrestling became intense. The pull to autonomy versus the pull to intimacy. Growth versus fallowness. Old wounds versus new healing. Freedom versus commitment. Choosing versus settling for. Leveling versus starting over. Hope versus despair. They were all there.

Early one morning we took a walk, moving through the shadows and listening to the crunch of pine cones beneath our shoes. The path wound uphill, getting steeper. I couldn't help but think how appropriate that was. Marriage has its own steep hills.

We slowed down and glanced at each other, as if we were looking for some affirmation in the other's face that the regeneration we were seeking in our relationship was really possible. It can be so difficult to believe in "what might be" when you're still embedded in "what is."

A line from Rilke played through my head: "Love consists in this, that two solitudes protect, and border, and salute each other."[22]

That's the relationship I ached to know. But I didn't know if it was possible. How do we become two solitudes, each contained and grounded in the self, while protecting, bordering, and saluting the other's deepest self? If such a thing could happen at all, it would require renegotiation; it would require that we become joint architects of a new marriage.

At the pinnacle of the hill, I paused to catch my breath. Sandy wandered ahead. "Look!" he called. Standing twenty yards ahead, he was pointing to a scarred tree stump. "Come closer."

I came closer. And there, growing in the center of the stump, was the green shoot of a new oak tree.

I don't know how long we stood side by side gazing at the new tree "hatching" from the old stump. All I know is that it seemed to me God was speaking eloquently once again about rebirth...a simple message about how life comes out of death and healing comes out of scars and wounds. The message said that rebuilding can happen after leveling. It said that hope is bigger than despair. It said so many things.

I looked at Sandy. Could we heal the wounds? Could I be my own person, with my own autonomy, following my own spiritual path, and still mesh and blend my life with his so that our souls touched? Would he allow it? Would I? Could we relate without either possessing the other? Could we honor the individual mystery in one another while at the same time singing the harmonics of intimacy? I wondered if we could love each other in such a supreme way. The tensions within me pulled almost unbearably.

As we continued on the trail in the woods, I reached a "combustion point." I felt a firming inside me of the truth, as if the knowing had begun to congeal in my soul. And not just the knowing but the desire to unfold it, the strength to follow it. A little act of creation happened right then. A little birth. An "eastering."

I slipped my hand into Sandy's. "I love you," I whispered. It was the first time in so long that I had said the words.

I felt his fingers tighten around mine. "I know. I love you too," he said.

And so we began to draw up our new blueprints.

GOD IN THE DARK

In the Bible darkness is often used as a metaphor for sin or a lack of God's presence. There are, however, references to darkness as a place where God dwells. "The Lord has set the sun in the heavens, but has said that he would dwell in thick darkness" (1 Kings 8:12). "He made darkness his covering around him" (Ps. 18:11).

God in the dark. Traditionally this imagery suggests the ultimate unknowability of God. But when I read it from within the dark layers of my cocoon, I perceived a meaning quite different. The verses filled me with an affirmation that God enters the thick darkness of every creature. A voice said to me, God suffers with you. God weeps with you. God lives your darkness. This is the recognition that turns our darkness into a shining thing.

Years earlier I had read some writings of Jürgen Moltmann, a German theologian who argued that God "experiences" our sufferings and grieves with us. Our soul is so connected with God, he said, that it's impossible for the divine Being not to share our anguish. Now suddenly the idea came alive to me.

Did God suffer? Was God capable of pain? Did God enter into our pain and powerlessness? Was God vulnerable? We're used to the all-powerful, invincible, triumphant God. But I was discovering the vulnerable God, the God who knows pain and oppression, who enters deeply into our wounds. The God who empties and waits.

That idea is expressed in a unique way in Flannery O'Connor's story "Parker's Back." In the story we meet handyman O. E. Parker, who has covered his body with tattoos in a bizarre attempt to lace his life together with a sense of harmony and meaning. O'Connor says that he's looking to turn his "spider web soul into a perfect arabesque of colors, a garden of trees and birds and beasts."[23] Through those tattoos he seeks wholeness, a united inner kingdom.

But the tattoos never deliver the wholeness he's seeking. He lives with the raging conflict of opposites within. In fact, O'Connor says that the display of birds and animals on his body seems to have "penetrated his skin and lived inside him in a raging warfare."

Parker is married to an intolerant, extremely religious, and equally annoying woman named Sarah, who hates his tattoos. The turning point of the story comes when Parker has a spiritual awakening while plowing. This propels him straight to the tattoo artist to get a picture of God tattooed on his back, the last bare spot on his body. Trembling with the power and beauty of his encounter, he picks out the face of a Byzantine Christ from the tattoo book and has the image placed indelibly on his flesh.

Afterward he sits in an alley, feeling Christ's eyes on his back, examining his soul. For the first time in his life he begins to know the "perfect arabesque of colors" within himself.

At nightfall he goes home, hoping that *this* tattoo will please his religious wife. When he takes off his shirt and shows Sarah the face, she screams, "Idolatry!" She grabs a broom and knocks him to the floor, then beats Parker's back until welts are raised, appearing simultaneously on the face of the tattooed Christ.

Parker's story is every person's story, for we're all searching for the "perfect arabesque of colors" inside—that which can lace us together in wholeness. We find it by discovering the image of God indelibly tattooed on our soul, faint and disfigured, perhaps, but present. As we go through the process of making it visible and whole, we suffer. When we're knocked off our feet by pain, the welts raised upon our soul are experienced by God, who is closer than our own skin.

A JOURNAL ENTRY

Throughout the spring and summer I lingered in the darkness, struggling to live inside my questions and hold the tensions creatively. One August day I opened my journal and wrote:

August 12. Today is my birthday. It makes me think of the new life I'm incubating and the Birth-day still to come. Sometimes it seems that life is a grace too severe, too vast, and too beautiful to receive. But I open my hands anyway. Today I'll talk to myself. I'll say, Accept life—the places it bleeds and the places it smiles. That's your most holy and human task. Gather up the pain and the questions and hold them like a child upon your lap. Have faith in God, in the movement of your soul. Accept what *is*. Accept the dark. It's okay. Just be true.

I'll say to myself, You're loved. Your pain is God's pain. Go ahead and embrace the struggle and chaos of it all, the splendor, the messiness, the wonder, the agony, the joy, the conflict. Love all of it.

I'll say to myself, Remember that little flame on the Easter candle. Cup your heart around it. Your darkness will become the light.

PASSAGE OF
EMERGENCE

CHAPTER 8

Unfurling New Wings

If I have inside me the stuff to make cocoons, maybe the stuff of butterflies is there too.

TRINA PAULUS

They that wait upon the Lord shall renew their strength.
They shall mount up with wings.

ISAIAH 40:31

I awoke one morning and went to my study before anyone else in the family was awake. I peered through the window at the red dawn spread low against the sky. I watched it a while, then sat down and propped my elbows on the pine of my roll-top desk. I ran a finger over the scarred place where I'd dropped a marble book end and gashed the surface. I thought about the scarred places of life, about the risk involved in birthing something new. I thought about the darkness, the misshapen moments we live through, the agonies that are tender and then fierce. I wondered if my quest was worth the pain.

The room was still; the silence was so thick that I could feel it drape around me like an old shawl. As I sat with it pulled against me, I became aware of something or someone else in the room. Something different—a faint rustling, a soft presence of some sort. I didn't know what it was.

Then all at once I knew. I raised my eyes to the pot of African violets on top of the desk. Sure enough, protruding above the rim of the pot was a wing—a startling black wing etched with blue and orange dots. It swayed back and forth.

I rose to my feet, awe palpable in my chest. *A butterfly!* She was almost too glorious to look at. Her new black wings were unfurled against the emerald green of the plant—translucent, like two dark blades of moving light. The chrysalis had opened!

In my study, in the gentleness of dawn, grace danced. The bright Mystery waltzed right through me.

For a long time I watched the butterfly with a joy that was close to tears. She made no attempt to fly; she just sat on the potting soil, pumping with her wings. She seemed to be readying herself for her new life.

Eventually my eyes sought out the empty cocoon, and I recalled the day I'd found it. Grace had danced then too. I remembered standing in the cold of February, staring at it; knowing somehow that God was speaking, that it was my soul incubating inside there. Now the cocoon was empty. I don't think I'd ever seen anything that filled me with such bravery.

I picked up the pot with the butterfly still inside, and carried it to the backyard. I set it on the ground, then pulled up a patio chair to wait. As the light grew, she moved from one leaf to another until she was at the top of the plant. She perched there a moment; then she flew.

She had been with me such a long time, curled in her cocoon, first in the yard and then on my desk. I'd watched over her. I'd loved her. Through her, God had watched over me, loved me, and taught me about the beauty and transformation of the soul. Now she flew.

As I watched her black wings dip and flutter through the morning, a verse moved silently in my thoughts. "Behold, I make all things new" (Rev. 21:5, KJV).

WOBBLY WINGS

When the time is right, the cocooned soul begins to emerge. Waiting turns golden. Newness unfurls. It's a time of pure, unmitigated wonder. Yet as we enter the passage of emergence, we need to remember that new life comes slowly, awkwardly, on wobbly wings.

I waited many long months before I felt newness begin to form, and many more before it began to unfold in my life. Gradually—oh, so gradually—my waiting season came to an end. The pain began to diminish bit by bit, as if it had peaked and now was giving way to something new. Many of the questions I'd lived with began to sprout little seeds of insight. Light trickled in. A new vision and way of life began to take shape not only in my head but in my heart and soul as well. It was as if I'd discovered a new room inside myself—a wider, more expansive place than I'd known before, but a room that had been there all along.

Changes—deep spiritual and psychological changes—started to make themselves known. Those changes took a lot of getting used to. The feeling of adjustment reminded me of the time I'd had my hair cut in a completely new look. Later that day, standing outside a store window, I caught the reflection of a woman. When I raised my arm, she raised hers. It gave me a start. For a split second I didn't recognize that the woman was me. Emergence is like that. We have to grow used to our newness even as we wear it. A new self is being born, and sometimes it takes a while to recognize her. She'll no doubt give us many starts.

I remember the space of time it took the black butterfly in my study to become airborne after emerging from the chrysalis. She gave herself time to unfurl her wings, pumping them back and forth. And her first flight wasn't exactly a study in elegance.

We need an adjustment time like that—a time for wobbly wings. It can go on for a long while. During this time we learn to be patient with ourselves. We give ourselves time to integrate the changes.

Just as important, we need to give people around us the same sort of time. One of the more difficult questions about spiritual transformation is, What about the people around me? If I grow and evolve, what will happen to my relationships with them?

We need to be prepared for other people's reactions to us and be patient with them too. While it may not be easy to get used to change in oneself, it can be even more difficult for those around us. After all, what happens when the Pleaser stops pleasing? What happens when Rapunzel stops looking to everyone else to rescue her and begins to climb out of the tower on her own? How do people respond when their favorite martyr ceases to sacrifice her life on the altar of duty? What's the reaction of others when the Tin Woodman recovers her heart and her real feelings and embraces her body and her sexuality? What happens when the Tinsel Star decides not to perform anymore? And what will people do when Chicken Little decides not to hide from life or truth but takes up her courage and goes out to meet it? When the dawn of a fuller spirituality appears and a new aspect of the True Self pushes its way up into the light, how will the people around us respond? Will they like our new wings?

Sometimes people are happy with our wings and support the unfurling. Sometimes, though, they're afraid of our wings and try to talk us back into the old larval life.

They can ignore our wings, tolerate them, attack them, applaud them, or bless them. They may even be changed by them. A transformation in one member of the family often creates transformation in others. Sometimes they go weave their own cocoons and join us. In *Hope for the Flowers*, the caterpillar Yellow was concerned about what would happen if she became a butterfly and her close friend Stripe remained a caterpillar. A gray-haired caterpillar told her, "If you change, you can fly and show him how beautiful butterflies are. Maybe he will want to become one too!"[1]

I encountered all sorts of reactions to the changes in my life. When the reaction was negative, I sometimes went into a temporary tailspin, regressed, and questioned everything.

The best advice I received on this subject was from an older woman who'd been through many cocoons and many pairs of wings. I told her, "People won't let me change." (As if people could really do that.) What I was actually saying was, "I'm afraid of people's reaction to my changes." The woman touched my cheek with her hand and said, "*Love your wings.*"

When we grow, there's nearly always an initial reaction of fear in those around us. It's understandable. When one person begins to change, it shakes up the safe, familiar order of things. If we rearrange the furniture inside ourselves, those who are accustomed to the old setup are bound to bump into things when they try to relate to us.

Sometimes people have designed their lives around our old behavior patterns. They may have become dependent on our being dependent on them. When Rapunzel becomes empowered, their world can be ruptured. Or they may have invested heavily in the need for our ideas and beliefs to flow in the same stream as theirs. When the Little Girl with a Curl finds her own voice, the currents of the relationship can suddenly swirl. People may have become so used to the Tin Woodman repressing her real feelings or dwelling in her head instead of her heart that when she begins to discover and express what's really inside, they're thrown by the truth.

If we cease being the Little Red Hen who does it all, a common reaction in others is bafflement, then anger. I recall the day Sandy came home from work and found my desk untouched, every bed in the house unmade, and tubes of paint and watercolor canvases spread across the dining-room table instead of dinner. "What have you been doing all day?" he asked in bewilderment.

"Playing," I said. "I gave myself the day off."

"But the beds aren't made."

I grinned. "I know. Isn't it wonderful?"

"But I'm hungry," he said, a tinge of annoyance in his voice.

I looked at him, my own anger on the verge of kicking in. It could have turned into a row, but the smudge of blue paint on my nose saved the day.

"I can't yell at you when you look that silly," he said.

We avoided an angry confrontation, but the incident pointed out to me how easily others can be derailed by changes, even tiny ones. It takes lots of talk, lots of time, and lots of understanding and adapting on both sides.

A man I know emerged from his chrysalis minus his old drivenness and need to be the professional star. He gave up his relentless agenda and adopted slower, more reflective, healing rhythms. To his surprise, his wife reacted bitterly. When busy people suddenly become still—when they begin to be not only human do-ings but human be-ings, as a friend of mine puts it—people around them can get aggravated. This man's wife, who had derived much of her own sense of worth from her husband's prominence, fought his changes for months.

If we begin to open up to new ways of experiencing our spirituality and expressing our authenticity, eyebrows may go up. When I left my Baptist roots to enter the Episcopal church, at least one friend was unhappy with my decision. I had a hard time convincing him that I was trying to balance my Baptist heritage with the sacramental and symbolic dimensions of worship. I was looking to walk a path that more closely mirrored where I was inside.

We simply need to give people time, accept their resistance, listen to their fears, reassure them, talk honestly with them, and go on quietly becoming our new self.

Above all, we need to love our wings.

CHRIST BORN IN YOU

As December approached, I sat by the wooden nativity set clustered under our Christmas tree and thought over the last year of my life, the year of waiting. Are we places of nativity too? I wondered.

Once, when I visited a monastery around Christmas, I passed a monk walking outside the church. "Merry Christmas," I said.

"May Christ be born in you," he replied.

I thought that a very peculiar greeting at the time, and I never forgot it. Now, all these years later, sitting beside the Christmas tree, I felt the impact of his words. The moment affirmed to me all over again what the real essence of spiritual transformation is all about: it's realizing more of our inner Christ-nature; it's discovering our soul and letting Christ be born from the waiting heart.

In the passage of emergence, as the birthing begins, the soul becomes a nativity. The whole Bethlehem pageant starts up inside us. An unprecedented new star shines in our darkness—a new illumination and awareness. God sends Wisdom to visit us, bearing gifts. The shepherding qualities inside us are summoned to help tend what's being born. The angels sing and a whole new music begins to float in the spheres. Some new living, breathing dimension of the life of Christ emerges with a tiny cry that says, I am.

One of the best parts of the whole drama is that it happens in the dung and the straw of our life, just as it happened in the dung and straw of Bethlehem. Birthing Christ is an experience of humility. Emerging to newness after the rigors of the cocoon isn't a spiritual "promotion." There's no presentation of a twenty-four-carat halo and a fancy new Christian persona without scuffs. If we're consumed with holy pride, convinced that we're spiritually "right" and on a higher plane than others, we haven't birthed a wider experience of the inner Christ but a new creation of the ego.

The Christ-life doesn't divorce us from our humanity: it causes us to embrace it. It makes us *more* human. It humbles us. Genuine transformation always connects us to our essential nature, both sacred *and* profane. When we go through its passages, we plumb the depths of our humanity. We become intimate with what lies inside—the wild and untamed, the orphaned and abused, the soiled and unredeemed. We hold our falseness in our hands and trace our fingers over the masks we wear, like a blind person feeling the unseen faces of those she wants to know. We stare into the sockets of our pain and glimpse the naked truth of who we are.

All this we bring with us into the new life. It ushers us into a new humility. Oh, yes, no doubt about it. We birth Christ on a pile of ordinary straw.

May Christ be born in you. That's the mystery at work as we unfurl new wings—even small, fragile wings.

There's a story about a young man who sought out a wise old man and asked, "What great blunder have you made?" The old man replied, "They called me a Christian, but I did not become Christ."

The seeker was perplexed. "You did not *become* Christ? Is one supposed to *become* Christ?"

The old man answered, "I kept putting distance between myself and him—by seeking, by praying, by reading. I kept deploring the distance, but I never realized that I was creating it."

"But," the seeker insisted, "is one supposed to *become* Christ?"

His answer: "No distance."[2] When there's no distance between us and our inner Christ, we're most human, most ourselves.

GIFTS OF THE SOUL

Through the transforming experience of contemplative waiting we're presented with gifts of the soul. These gifts are the most important we can receive, for they're the *expressions* of the Christ-life, the True Self, which is beginning to unfold itself in our lives. Jungian analyst and Presbyterian clergyman Murray Stein writes,

> When the soul awakens at midlife and presents its gifts, life is permanently marked by the inclusion of them. Taken in, they become the hallmark of your life, the core of your uniqueness. Refused, they can haunt your days and may undermine all your toiling. I cannot specify what the gift of soul to you will be at midlife. I can only suggest that when it is presented it be received.[3]

We're called upon to receive the gifts of the True Self, to open our hands.

Let's be aware, however, that the Christ-life is born into each life in unique ways. The gifts that your soul presents may be different from the gifts that my soul presents. We need to allow for the differences, as well as for variance in timetables. Spiritual experiences aren't meant to be homogeneous, only harmonious—not in unison, but in unity.

If all souls developed in cookie-cutter fashion, we would have spirituality by duplication rather than by waiting and transformation. Yet the tendency exists among Christians to want everybody to be at the same place at the same time. You know how it goes. Everybody should be actively ministering. (But even Jesus had seasons of waiting as well as ministering.) Everybody should be happy. (But even Jesus was at times sad, anguished, and in pain.) Everybody should be relating to God in the same way. (But even Jesus related to God in different ways—sometimes inwardly, sometimes outwardly.) What would happen if we allowed people to unfurl their wings and move into the fullness of being each in her own time and way?

With this in mind, I want to turn attention to some of the specific gifts of soul that can manifest themselves in our lives.

Delight

When the True Self breaks through, a new and impassioned approach to life often makes itself known. We tap into an inner radiance that I call *delight*. I'm speaking of a unique kind of response to life that can coexist with our most painful realities. I'm speaking of the joy of saying yes to life in the core of our being.

I believe that the capacity to delight in life is deeply carved by our waiting. "When I planted my pain in the field of patience," wrote Kahlil Gibran, "it bore fruit of happiness."[4]

Delight comes by way of scars. One of my favorite stories is a variation of an old tale that circulated through New England in the nineteenth century.[5] An insect egg was deposited into an apple tree on a farm in Connecticut. One day the tree was struck by lightning and fell to the ground. The farmer took the apple wood and made it into a table, which sat in the kitchen for many years. One day he heard a strange sound, like gnawing, coming from the wood. It kept up for weeks, until finally a beautiful winged bug emerged through a scar in the table, opened its wings, and flew about the kitchen in a little dance of joy, delighting (it seemed) in the long-awaited experience of being alive.

Delight comes that way—wounds, waiting, and finally wings. It gnaws out through the scar.

One summer, while Sandy and I were staying on Harbor Island in South Carolina, we walked on the beach, coming to the point where the ocean curves into Helena Sound. There we waded into the surf. Suddenly a bottle-nosed dolphin splashed out of the water twenty yards away, spiraling into the air. He dived back into the water, then came rising out of it again in a burst of spray. It was an exhilarating moment for us, as it seemed to be for him. Like the bug emerging from the table, the dolphin seemed to be delighting in the wonder of being alive.

But do you know what captured me most of all? Across the back of the dolphin was a large silver scar. He had been wounded, perhaps through an encounter with a predator or the blades of a boat. I thought to myself, There it is again, the echo of one of God's deepest truths: delight can emerge from and exist along with our scars.

Delight can become a way of life, a way of journeying. There's a saying, "Religion is not to be believed, but danced."[6] I like this idea, for it shifts the emphasis from our endless pursuit of religious knowledge back to the dimension of *living* our religion in such a way that it becomes a dance, a celebration in which we open our arms and say yes to life.

At times I've interrupted my spiritual journey by lingering in a corner of the dance floor watching others dance or by studying the movements of the dance in a book. The point of the spiritual life is that you dance the music God pipes in *you*.

Let's return for a moment to Dorothy's adventures in Oz. When she lands there, she meets the witch of the north who is depicted as a white-haired, wrinkle-faced old crone of a woman. She presents Dorothy with a pair of shiny silver (not red) slippers. Dorothy takes off her old leather shoes and puts them on. Soon she learns to click her heels and *dance* the journey instead of plodding it. She changes shoes.

We're also called from plodding to dancing. The True Self presents us with dancing shoes. Like Dorothy, we take off our heavy leather shoes and lace on the new slippers.

God showed me a joyful new way of dancing life. It began when I discovered the metaphor of God as child. In this image of the Divine, I found the delighting, playful Presence who pulls us into life, into gladness, into the fullness of being.

We're all familiar with Jesus' saying that we must become like little children, (Matt. 18:3) but I'd never come to terms with the idea that God did the very same thing. *God* became a little child. Our hearts warm at the thought of the baby at Bethlehem, but do we really *relate* to God as child? I had related mostly to an "adult" God.

Then I happened upon some vivid words by Mechtild: "I, God, am your playmate! I will lead the child in you in wonderful ways for I have chosen you."[7] At first the image shocked me. God as *playmate?* Wasn't God supposed to be really serious? Did God actually want to *play* with me? Incredible! The image sparked the same sense of incongruence I'd felt the first time I visited Sandy's family. Midway into my visit the doorbell rang. I opened the door to find two little boys about seven, one with a ball and bat. "Can Gramp come out and play?" they asked. (Sandy's eighty-year-old grandfather lived with them.) I was surprised at the question, but not nearly as surprised as when Gramp put on his cap and followed them out.

Now the image of God as playmate shattered my over-grown-up seriousness and began to liberate the joyful child in me. I became more simple, wonder-filled, and playful.

During this time I attended a workshop called "The Inner Child." I wanted to know more about the childlikeness that Jesus urged us to discover and to explore this idea of God as a playmate. Twenty adults were given paper and colored chalk and asked to draw a particular childhood experience. I drew myself sitting in my sandbox building a castle. And suddenly, out of nowhere, a lost memory floated back to me.

I was around five. I'd built a sandcastle in my sandbox and was searching for a flower or a pebble with which to crown the top of it. I walked to the mimosa tree and concocted one of those imaginary adventures for which children are famous: I imagined that there was a rainbow hanging upside down from a tree limb and that if I reached up and touched it, the castle in my sandbox would turn into a real castle. So I got on my tiptoes and pretended to touch the rainbow. Then I skipped around the tree, celebrating the event, being who I was, playing with God, singing some deep song of delight.

As the memory faded and I returned to the present, I was deeply affected—touched in an all-but-forgotten place. I sensed that those childhood moments of building a castle, touching an imaginary rainbow, and dancing around the tree held inside them the most delight I had ever known or ever could know. It was that child who connected me to the radiant center of life.

There in the workshop I thought about the book I had grown up to read: *The Interior Castle,* in which Teresa of Avila said that the soul is a castle through which we move to get to the Center. In an odd way, it seemed to me that the magical scenario I had concocted as a child was really true after all. When we touch the place where the rainbow hangs upside down—the inner child inside us—we find the *real* castle, the soul's castle.

The workshop leader asked us to acknowledge the child we had drawn as a real part of us and give him or her a name. Before I even really thought I picked up my crayon and wrote "Delight" beneath my picture.

She was part of the new life that was emerging from the cocoon—a part that was learning how to play with God, to lace on dancing slippers and skip with God in the pure experience of being alive.

Gradually I learned to "go delighting." I began to laugh more, ride horses, climb up into my children's treehouse, tussel in the grass with my beagles, and throw unexpected picnics on the den floor. When I did those sorts of things, finding ways to connect to God as a playmate, I was living in the castle that Delight built.

In this castle we recapture our lost spontaneity, which is the stuff delight is made of. Recently my sixteen-year-old son and I were leaving the grocery store. I shuffled along, preoccupied, as he pushed the grocery cart into the parking lot. (I was wearing my leather plodding shoes.) Much of the day I'd been trapped in a solemn parade of details. "Hey, Mama! Do you want a ride?" Bob asked.

As a child he'd stood in the front of the grocery cart while I pushed it to the car. Now he was pushing the cart and inviting *me* to ride.

I was about to say, "Certainly not. Mothers do *not* ride grocery carts through the parking lot of Winn Dixie, even when it's practically deserted," when Delight intervened. She stepped into the cart with me. As we sped off, the solemn, suffocating tone of the day evaporated almost instantly. I felt opened up and breathed into once again by God.

In the Bible the word *joy* can be translated "delight." When Jesus said that he wanted his joy to be in us and our joy to be full (John 15:11), he was also saying that he wanted his delight to be in us. He wanted our delight to be full. Finding the inner child, Delight, plumps and widens our joy. She lives in all of us.

She's a precious gift to the soul that connects us back to God as our original playmate. She tickles our frozen places and frees us to laughter, exuberance, simplicity, and spontaneous moments that extract the essence of the True Self from deep inside.

The Mothering of God

One of the more beautiful gifts of the soul that I discovered was coming to experience God not only through the image of father but also through the image of mother. (God keeps getting bigger!)

Ann Belford Ulanov, professor of psychiatry and religion at Union Theological Seminary, encourages us to look carefully at our pictures of God. "The pictures we have of God, both our individual pictures and our group pictures, will show us unmistakeably what we leave out in ourselves and what we must look at."[8]

What *is* missing in us and how *is* it connected to what we've left out of our individual and group pictures of God? It seems to me that we've left out the feminine—the principle that's universally recognized as the one that draws us into intimacy and relatedness, that opens, lets go and lets be, nourishes, receives, reconciles, and connects us.

The Bible says that God created us male and female in the divine image (Gen. 1:27). In other words, God's image isn't one gender nor the other; it encompasses the pattern of both men and women. As I discovered that God is like a mother as well as a father, I awoke in a fresh way to the warm, gentle, nurturing Presence of God, to the one who gathers us, as Jesus said, like a mother hen gathers a chick under her wing (Matt. 23:37). "We have to hear of God's feminine tenderness towards us before we will...take up relationship,"[9] notes author Lorna Green. Opening up to the mothering of God unearthed feelings of love from caves deep in my soul, caves that I had never explored.

Not only does the mother metaphor bring us to a new ground of intimacy with God, it can also help us respond to a world at deep risk. It helps us find a new vision of caring for the world and helps us awaken to the primacy of relationship over power, embrace tenderness, and lovingly endure the labor pains necessary to bring about forgiveness, solidarity, and community.

The mothering of God reveals to us the God who suffers and feels and waits in order to create, birth, and heal. When we relate to this image of God, we're more apt to make ourselves vulnerable, to incubate what's dark, care for the wounded, the broken, and the alienated—the motherless in our world.

I've wondered, too, if including the feminine in our picture of God might also help balance what has become a one-sided spirituality. Can it help us balance the logical, masculine intellect with the intuitive, feminine heart? Can it help us balance the dogma and theological approaches of religion with a revaluation of story and personal experience? Might it allow our feminine being to be as important as our masculine doing? Could a feminine metaphor of God help teach us to slowly grow the life of the Spirit inside us? Who better than a mothering God to teach us birth?

A Return to the Earth

One of the more unexpected gifts that I began to discover was the wedding of my soul with creation. It was no longer a matter of gazing at a mountain and being reminded that here is God's footstool. No, it was something else—a deepening sense of oneness with the earth as the place where God cradles and grows life, where everything is contained, connected, and nourished. It was as if I were a thread being woven into what Hildegard called "the web of the universe."[10]

In the book *The Color Purple* the character of Celie expressed it like this: "One day when I was sitting quiet and feeling like a motherless child, which I was, it come to me: that feeling of being part of everything, not separate at all. I knew that if I cut a tree, my arm would bleed."[11]

This awareness begins what I can only call a return to the earth. The return is sometimes sparked when we start to heal the Tin Woodman inside us and return to our bodies. If we deny and mistreat our physical bodies, we tend to deny and mistreat the body of mother earth. When we begin to reverence the body as the container of the soul, finding a deep reverence for the Holy within creation is not far behind.

In our return to the earth we start to experience within creation what Gerard Manley Hopkins called the "dearest freshness deep down things."[12] We're grazed by the truth that every bird in a nest, every gurgle of a brook, every coral in the sea is God's beloved. Hildegard said that God adores creation and creation adores God. She pleaded that the earth not be injured, for earth's injury is an injury to God.

My spirituality went through a metamorphosis in which I started to care—*really care*—about how I related to creation, from the beetle crawling on my kitchen floor to the nuclear missiles my government stockpiles. I began to feel passionately about bombs, the slaughter of whales, the destruction of rain forests, holes in the ozone, polluted beaches, toxic waste, smogged air. These things were the desecration of God's art—the scarring of my own mother's face.

While visiting Springbank Retreat Center one weekend, I took a walk. In a rare moment God seemed to whisk my vision clean. I felt enveloped by the beauty of what I saw, by the suddenness of love welling up in me.

I sat down beside what I've come to call *the* tree. It's the largest, most ancient tree I've ever seen. A live oak, its serpentine limbs travel to the sky while its moss dips to the earth. It's nearly impossible to sit by this tree and not feel your heart waking up. Before long my soul became so full that I wrote my feelings on some scraps of paper I found in my pocket, composing what I now realize was a love letter.

> Dear God, I love this tree. I love the light filtering through the moss and the leaves. I love all your earth songs—the breeze rustling through the grass, the rhythm of crickets, the beating of wings.
>
> I love the rain water in the bird bath and the dragonflies that flit over it. I love the air so laden with moisture that the dew rains out of the tree and bathes my face. I love the artistic little prayers that the spiders weave through the woods. I love the way you blend daylight into darkness, how dusk softens the sharp edges of the world. I love the way the moon changes shape every night. I love the slope of your hills— horizons inside and out. I feel that I'm part of it, that it's part of me.
>
> Here, surrounded and permeated by your creation, I feel *you*. I feel life. I know myself connnected. O God, is there anything you've made that *can't* pour life and healing into me? When I think of the simplicity and extravagance of creation, I want to bend down and write the word *yes* across the earth so that you can see it.

Attunement

One of the more delicate gifts of soul that can come from the chrysalis is a refined attunement to the here-and-now. We learn how to be genuinely present to life.

Jesus implied that the kingdom is now (Luke 17:21; Matt. 3:2). Contemplatives tell us that this moment is *it*. Now is all you really have. It's the only place where you and life intersect.

Someone brought to my attention that the words *nowhere* and *now here* have the same arrangement of letters; the letters are merely separated by a small space in the latter. Likewise, a fine space separates us from experiencing life as *nowhere* or *now here*.

A lot of us go about not here at all. We're disengaged from life happening right now. One afternoon I got in my car, rehashing something that had happened earlier that morning, to run an errand. Ten minutes later I found myself in front of Ann's school, where I went five days a week to pick her up. The problem was that this was Saturday and I'd been on my way to the dry cleaner. I felt foolish, but I learned how completely cut off I could be from the present. I had been nowhere.

At other nowhere times I replayed moments I'd already lived, like television reruns. Minister John Claypool said in a sermon that the past is a great place to visit, but he wouldn't want to live there. I agree. To constantly relive the past is to miss out on the present.

More frequently, though, I was preoccupied with the future, with where and how I would spend the next moments. I projected myself into unlived time, *preparing* to live rather than living. "Our eyes become so focused on goals," wrote Sam Keen, "that we forget to wonder in the presence of a rose."[13]

Remember that wonderful old slogan, "Life is what happens when you're making other plans"? My friend Betty has an equally priceless one on her desk: "Enjoy life. This is not a dress rehearsal." Such reminders shock me back to the reality of the moment. They say to me, what makes you think life happens on *tomorrow's* stage? This is no rehearsal. This is *it*. Live it now!

We spend time reliving history or devising the future much more than we think. Some of that is important, but when we "live" in those realms, investing most of our consciousness there, we don't dwell in the present moment in a deep way. We lose touch with the nowness of life; we lose touch with soul.

After a while this disengagement creates a sense of spiritual boredom, even though we're living busy, goal-oriented lives crammed with people, events, and places. This boredom comes from a lack of attunement with and a disconnection from the place where life is most vital and real: the Eternal Now.

The waiting of the cocoon helped me begin to recenter my consciousness more on the here and now. It routed my ego-dominated need to think mostly in terms of memory and anticipation and taught me to be where I was, taught me that time isn't a straight line along which we travel, but a deep dot in which we dwell.

It can be difficult trying to relate to time. These days its pressure weighs on us almost constantly. It drives us; we arrange our lives around it. One of the great curses of our age is living *by* time rather than *in* time.

There are two words for time in the Bible: *chronos* and *kairos*. When *chronos* dominates, we live by time. Life is experienced as chonology, as one thing happening after another. This is a linear way of thinking about time, with the relentless cadence of tick-tock, tick-tock. The sound takes up residence inside us. Our hearts fall in sync. Why, we even refer to our hearts as "tickers." Sam Keen suggests that when we live by *chronos* "we march to the beat of an alien pacemaker."[14]

When *kairos* dominates, we live *in* time, in the deep dot. Life is experienced as opportunity. *Kairos* is full time, real time. It requires dwelling in the moment so completely that the possibility of life opens up to us.

Spiritual transformation enables us to move from *chronos* to *kairos*. We start to tap the immediacy of life again. We crack open the moment to discover the treasure of beingness. The present moment becomes the Communion bread that's broken to reveal the presence of Christ.

In his spiritual classic *Abandonment to Divine Providence* Jean-Pierre de Caussade wrote that the single most important concern of the soul is to seek and accept the present moment. "The present moment is always overflowing with immeasureable riches, far more than you are able to hold," he wrote. He was insistent that our passing moments aren't trivial but "enclose the entire kingdom of holiness."[15]

Is this what William Blake was getting at when he wrote "Auguries of Innocence"?

> To see a World in a Grain of Sand
> And Heaven in a Wild Flower,
> Hold Infinity in the palm of your hand,
> And Eternity in an hour.[16]

I once read a Hasidic story about a teacher who was said to have lived an unusually abundant life. After his death one of his pupils was asked, "What was most important to your teacher?" The pupil replied, "Whatever he happened to be doing at the moment."[17] He had come home to the Eternal Now.

My mentor, Beatrice, wrote, "Be what you're actually doing at the moment." If you're plowing, plow fully in the moment, with your whole mind and heart—in other words, "become plowing."[18]

One day I saw a butterfly land on the petal of a pink impatiens and begin to drink the nectar. Because I'm now incurably attached to these creatures, I paused to watch. I inched closer until it was in reach of my fingertips. To my surprise, it allowed me to reach out and brush its wing with my finger.

Later I understood that I'd been able to touch the butterfly only because it was utterly intent on and connected with what it was doing in that moment. It's an irony, of course, that it happened on the petal of an *impatiens*, which is exactly the stage where most of us live our lives.

In the cocoon we can learn this kind of attunement. We can emerge like the butterfly extracting the nectar from the moment. We can learn to center our awareness in the present so that it becomes *kairos*, the moment spilling over with life and God. That's the heart of contemplative living.

There are perhaps three stages in contemplative awareness or attunement. In the first *we hear the words but not the music*. As I was leaving a concert of Handel's *Messiah*, I overheard two women talking. "Wasn't that the most glorious music you ever heard?" one asked. The other replied, "Frankly, I didn't like the repetition of words in the lyrics."

I walked away appalled. One woman had heard the music; the other had heard nothing but the words. That's often the way it is with the concert of life: some of us hear only the words. We have a grasp of outer things. We know the "right" answers, the "correct" lines, the "proper" behavior and wording for life. We live by rote, mouthing the words, unaware of the depth of melody flowing inside. At this level we tend to live *by* time, so mired in *chronos* that we don't even realize that there's *kairos* in the world.

As we grow in contemplative awareness, however, *we hear the words and the music*. We wake to inner things, to the interior life, to the glorious lilt of the soul. We begin to discover a new horizon of consciousness that brings us in contact with the here and now. We pause now and then to hear the deep-down music God plays within and around us. We're like one who sits in the audience and listens appreciatively.

Finally, in the third stage of attunement, *we become the music*. In "Four Quartets" T. S. Eliot speaks of "music heard so deeply/that it is not heard at all, but you are the music."[19] As we enter the deeper levels of contemplation, we cease *hearing* the music and *become* the music. We leave our chair in the audience and enter the symphony.

Becoming the music is the height of beingness. It happens when we dwell in the now with such openness and wholeheartedness that we merge with the moment, with the Presence hidden within it.

A monk at the Abbey of Gethsemani seemed to be expressing this state when he told me that the aim of the spiritual life is finding union with God through contemplation of everything around you, and then of divinity. "This is the God-life in the here and now," he said. "It breaks in upon us. Our hope is to make it more and more continuous."

We can move through all three of these stages of attunement in a single hour, or never budge from the first stage in an entire lifetime. Some days I hear only the words. Some days I hear the music. My moments of *being* music are rare, however. When we do taste such moments, we're left with the feeling that *this* is the way life is supposed to be. That's the sense I had when I sat beneath the mossy tree at Springbank. As I became more and more present to the music of those moments, I not only heard the rise and fall of God in the notes but I *entered* them. For a brief time I felt like music.

Authenticity

In another Hasidic tale, a rabbi named Zusya died and went to stand before the judgment seat of God. As he waited for God to appear, he grew nervous thinking about his life and how little he had done. He began to imagine that God was going to ask him, "Why weren't you Moses or why weren't you Solomon or why weren't you David?" But when God appeared, the rabbi was surprised. God simply asked, "Why weren't you Zusya?"[20]

The spiritual journey is one of becoming real. Waiting can offer us the gift of authenticity. It can help us give birth to a new way of being true to ourselves. As we wait, we discover that it's okay—really okay—not only to imagine who we truly are inside but to say who we are, welcome who we are, and even *be* who we are.

When I first began writing, I couldn't admit to anyone—even myself—that I was a writer. People would call me on the phone while I was writing and ask, "What are you doing?" I would say, "Oh, nothing." After a while I admitted (gulp!) that I was writing, but I made light of it, as if the identity belonged to someone else and I was borrowing it. Later, as I came to my authenticity as a writer, I simply answered, "I'm writing."

Owning my writerhood was a slow process. That's how it is with the new selfhood taking shape within. We own it a little at a time; bit by bit the realness shines through.

In the fall of that year I tossed my easel and sketch pad in the car and drove to Kanuga Episcopal Center in the Blue Ridge Mountains. On the way I passed a billboard advertising Coca-Cola. "The real thing," it said. I smiled.

I'd spent a lot of my life wearing masks to fit the occasion, being everything to everybody even if that meant being someone other than myself. Now, after long months of passionate waiting and labor pains, it seemed that I was birthing more of my True Self. The real thing.

At Kanuga I walked to the edge of the thirty-acre lake surrounded by mountain laurel. I set up my easel, pulled out my charcoal pencils, and looked about for a scene to sketch. There were so many—the sun nesting on the mountains like a small red bird, ducks floating on the lake, trees the color of pumpkins.

I began to draw, but none of those lovely scenes around me. I drew something inside me instead. I sketched a mother cradling a newborn baby against her breast. I drew until the remaining light had nearly seeped away. Then I stared at the picture. In an instant of recognition I knew that God was the mother in the picture and I was the child. Yet I also felt that I was the mother and God was the child.

Gazing at the sketch on my easel, I felt the realness of the tiny new creature inside me. That moment liberated a freedom not only to say who I was and what I believed but to actually *be* this person God and I had birthed and would go on birthing.

Several nights later I dreamed a similar message. I awoke while it was still dark and wrote the dream down.

I'm walking around a circular lake. In the water I see the reflection of a tree that's filled with butterflies. I walk on and on, struggling through lots of bramble until I find the actual tree growing beside the water. I stand beneath it with a sense of awe. I realize that I'm supposed to purchase the tree. At first I don't know if I have enough money. I must reach deep down into all my pockets before I find enough money to buy the tree.

The tree full of butterflies spoke to me of the authenticity beginning to unfold inside me, the wobbly new wings opening up. I was terribly unfinished. I had certainly not "arrived" and never would. (Do any of us ever?) I had days when I packed up my wings and didn't give authenticity a thought.

Still, there was *some* breakthrough of newness in my life. The Little Red Hen was learning how to love herself and be in touch with her soul, to be here now, to become Delight and play with God. The Little Girl with a Curl was learning to author her own life, to be true to herself, to be real. Gradually Rapunzel was discovering her God-given empowerment and autonomy. The Tinsel Star was continuing to encounter God's love, which helped her accept herself and her humanity and lessened her need to perform and achieve. Chicken Little was learning how to risk entering life more abundantly and fully. The Tin Woodman was returning to the earth of her own body, gradually finding a new wholeness for the divisiveness that kept body and soul separated.

At first, as my dream suggested, the realization of the new isn't substantive; it's a mere reflection in the deep pool of ourselves— something there, but not yet actualized. We have to struggle through a lot of inner "bramble" to get to the real tree. I tripped over fears about what it would mean to really be my authentic self. What if I broke some of the "rules of life" I'd grown up with? What if others rejected my newness?

I came to realize that I needed to purchase the butterfly tree. In other words, I needed to make the new life—this new landscape in my soul—my own. In dreams money is often symbolic of energy, the currency of life. God seemed to be offering a suggestion that I dig down into the deeper pockets of myself to find the spiritual energy to own the newness that was unfolding.

We find this spiritual energy by returning again and again to God at our center and making time for the soul. The soul must be continually nourished or, like the body, it becomes weak and malnourished. Without spiritual food there's little energy for the inner movement so necessary for living deeply in the spiritual life. Many times we starve our souls, although we wouldn't dream of starving our bodies. Or we offer them only shallowness—a spiritual "junk food."

The soul craves experiences that offer it the rich depths of God. Silence, solitude, holy leisure, simplicity, prayer, journaling, the Eucharist, rituals that touch the space of Mystery, symbols and images, the Bible, laughter, delight in the divine Presence, deep encounters with creation, and the merciful coming together of human hearts. All these feed the soul, producing energy for living the transformed life.

When I fail to feed my soul, I soon notice that I have less strength for living authentically. At times my energy becomes depleted. Weakened, I'm more apt to revert to old patterns. That's when I need to return to the deeper pockets and replenish my soul. There's truth in Psalm 23: allowing oneself to be led by still waters really does restore the soul.

Owning the butterfly tree is a continuous process. Just as we constantly give birth to a more authentic, Christ-like self, we need to constantly tap the spiritual energy necessary to nourish it.

Compassion

"Once you are a butterfly you can *really* love—the kind of love that makes life new."[21] These words from *Hope for the Flowers* point us to the consummate gift that the soul presents: compassion.

Meister Eckhart was adamant that compassion was the aim of all spiritual growth. I think that's one reason I like him so much; he had a big heart. He said, "If you were in an ecstasy as deep as that of St. Paul and there was a sick man who needed a cup of soup, it were better for you that you returned from the ecstasy and brought the cup of soup for love's sake."[22]

As the True Self is born within us, the initial movement of soul is from the collective "they" to the ground of an authentic "I." That's holy ground, yet God calls us to a ground even holier: God calls us from the authentic "I" toward a compassionate "we."

As we emerge from the chysalis, the illusion of separateness is shattered. We discover that God so loved the world that God gave us each other. We enter a vibrant knowing that we're one with every creature.

In the contemplation of our waiting hearts, we so encounter the life of God in the soul that we begin to gradually draw from a new set of values and orientations—those of compassion.

This movement is portrayed in an enchanting little book, *Tales of a Magic Monastery*:

> I sat there in awe as the old monk answered our questions. Though I am usually shy,...I found myself raising my hand. "Father, could you tell us something about yourself?" He leaned back. "Myself?" he mused. There was a long pause.
>
> "My name used to be Me. But now it's You."[23]

Through our suffering, waiting, and growing we tap more of the compassionate-we experience. It's hard to do unless we first find our authentic self and become an I. Teilhard de Chardin tells us that the essential aspiration is "to be united, that is to become the other, while remaining oneself."[24] It's only because we've found our individual boundaries and truth that we can cross them to find a genuine oneness with others (and not lose ourselves in the process).

What does it mean to experience the compassionate we? The answer becomes clear when we look at the word *compassion*, which literally means *com* ("with") *passion* ("suffering"). To have compassion is to suffer with. It's not feeling a detached pity but sharing the pain. Moving toward the compassionate experience makes us available with empathy to another.

Thomas Kelly put it beautifully: "One might say we become cosmic mothers tenderly caring for all."[25] Becoming a "cosmic mother" is very similar to Charles de Foucauld's idea of being a "universal brother" (and, I would add, a universal sister). It means to relate to the world in such a way that we see others not as strangers but as part of us. This relatedness allows us to walk with them in their deep and wounded places.

I gathered with a group of women one Sunday morning at Springbank. As we sat in a circle in the old log house, Kathleen, one of the Dominican sisters who lives at the center, led us in worship. She asked us to name those who were suffering, those whose cries were echoing in the world and inside our own hearts.

We named the homeless, the hungry, the abused, the rejected, the poor, the lonely, the sick, the grieving, the fragmented, the worn down, the defeated, and those wounded by power, oppressed, and made inferior. As I looked at the women around me, compassion was shining in their faces and filling their eyes. It was as if *they* were the homeless and the hungry, those wounded by power and made inferior. They were every suffering man and woman and child. I wanted to clasp them to me and smooth their hair and tell them over and over that I was there with them; I was there, God help me, I was there.

In a sense we were a little group of cosmic mothers and universal sisters hearing the cries of the world, catching the tears of others, and blending them with our own.

That experience went to my core. It woke me up in a new way to the silent thundering of pain around me. It taught me the depth of feeling and connection it takes to draw the suffering human being to one's breast in a real act of healing.

Not long afterward I met a thirty-two-year-old single woman during a layover in the Charlotte airport. She was a stranger, but because we both had two hours to wait, we fell into conversation at a corner table in the airport restaurant. We found that we were both writers traveling to the same conference.

During breaks in the conference we talked as well. One evening she told me about the devastating physical and emotional abuse she had suffered as a child. "I've never known what it's like to be loved. My father deserted me, and my mother never touched me except to hit me. No one in my whole life has ever said to me the words, 'I love you.'" Her voice broke off into sobs. I felt them reverberate inside me like tiny explosions.

Suddenly I clasped her to me and told her, "I'm here with you. *I* love you." And I did. I had loved her at Springbank before I even met her.

Once divine compassion wakes us and stretches out its tender arms inside us, we're never the same again. We're compelled to suffer with, wait with, cry with those around us. We want to relieve their pain as much as we're able. And by relieving theirs, we relieve God's. We do it for no reason except that compassion asks it.

Another of Eckhart's wonderful sayings is that love "has no why."[26] We can't always separate out our motives and respond purely from love. There are often hidden agendas that grow out of the little game of what's-in-it-for-me? Yet real compassion flows from God within—from plenitude, not ego or neediness. Such compassion is always born within, not imposed or mandated from without.

Jesus was walking, talking compassion. As we're able to live more of our True Self, that's what we become as well. We become Christ, showing an uncanny interest in the poor, the excluded, the despised, and the least. We find ourselves sitting by a Samaritan well, more interested in breaking down barriers than in religious do's and don'ts. We wrap a towel around our waist and wash the dirtiest feet around, proclaiming the preposterous message that there are no more lords and servants, no more ranks and hierarchies, but that we're all equal friends, serving one another. We amaze ourselves by coming to the rescue of an adulterous woman about to be stoned. We forgive the very ones who drive nails into our hands and feet.

The coming of the True Self tosses us into the wreckage of the world and asks us to bind up what wounds we can and do our small part to recreate a planet of community and justice, where there is fullness of life for everyone.

Such a vision becomes real only as compassion inflames one small heart after another. In his book *Night*, Elie Wiesel wrote about his horrifying childhood experiences in a Nazi concentration camp.[27] Having gone without food or drink for three days, thousands of Jews were driven out of their barracks at dawn into a thickly falling snow and herded into a field. Forbidden to sit or even move much, they stood in line until evening, waiting for a train that would take them deeper into Germany. The snow drifted in a layer on their shoulders.

Finally, their thirst intolerable, one man suggested that they eat the snow, but they weren't allowed by the guards to bend over. The person in front of that man agreed to let him eat the snow that had accumulated on the back of his shoulders, however. That act spread through the line until there, in a frozen field, what had been individuals struggling with their separate pain became a community sharing their suffering together.

The waiting heart arrives at the truth of compassion: that we'll survive as a human family only as we're willing, one by one, to become the place of nourishment for our brother and sister. We'll survive as we cease being individuals struggling alone with our pain and become instead a community sharing our suffering in a great and holy act of compassion.

COME TO THE EDGE

Today I walked across the Anderson College campus to the dogwood tree where I discovered the cocoon. As I gazed at it, I found myself hoping that one day soon another cocoon would hang upon its limbs. The world needs such expressions of grace to remind us that when the heart waits, the Great Mystery begins.

I lingered at the tree, remembering the long, difficult passages of my journey. I remembered the quiet call to wait, the ongoing confrontation with my false selves, the unending letting go, the still prayers, the sacred questions, the dazzling dark, the trembling new. I stood there, two years after my midlife pain had begun, and celebrated what the journey had given me, what it had taught me. Every brightness, every tear, every grace, every turn, every truth, every homecoming, however small.

The sun was behind the tree, coming through the leaves in little pinpricks of light. I smiled at it, feeling the height and depth and weight of my journey. "Yes, it's tough, it's tough, that goes without saying," wrote Annie Dillard. "But isn't waiting itself a wonder. . .?"[28] Yes, it *was* a wonder—a tough and sacred wonder.

I reminded myself that there would be other cocoons in life. Spiritual growth has no boundaries. My journey would spiral on, for there were wingless places in me—life and soul still unborn.

As I turned my feet toward home, a childhood memory returned to me. It was the year that I discovered a nest of baby birds in the branch of a pine tree near my house. I visited the nest almost daily throughout the summer. One day as I watched, a young bird hopped to the edge of the nest and perched there. I seemed to understand even then that I'd happened upon a moment of utter rarity; the small bird was about to take what was perhaps its maiden flight.

I braced, feeling my heart thudding in my chest. Come on, little bird. Come on. But the bird didn't move. It seemed afraid, petrified. Suddenly the mother bird appeared. She gave her youngling a gentle push, and off it flew. The bird soared over the treetops.

As the memory evaporated into the autumn afternoon, I walked on, hope rising in me. Hope for you and me and the journeys we undertake. Hope that we would trust our waiting hearts enough to risk entering them, that we would listen for the Voice that bids us come to the edge, and that we would welcome the gentle push of God, who is both our wings and the wind that bears them up.

Notes

CHAPTER 1

1. T. S. Eliot, "East Coker," *The Complete Poems and Plays, 1909-1950* (New York: Harcourt, Brace and World, 1971), 126.
2. Elizabeth O'Conner, *Our Many Selves* (New York: Harper & Row, 1971), 3.
3. Eliot, "The Love Song of J. Alfred Prufrock," *The Complete Poems and Plays*, 4–5.
4. Janice Brewi and Anne Brennan, *Mid-life: Psychological and Spiritual Perspectives* (New York: Crossroad, 1982), 19.
5. C. G. Jung, "Stages of Life," *The Structure and Dynamics of the Psyche*, vol. 8 of *Collected Works of C. G. Jung*, trans. R. F. C. Hull (Princeton, N.J.: Princeton University Press, 1960), para. 783.
6. John Shea, *Stories of God: An Unauthorized Biography* (Chicago: Thomas More Press, 1978), 29.
7. Alan Jones, *Journey into Christ* (San Francisco: Harper & Row, 1977), 52.
8. Frieda Fordham, *An Introduction to Jung's Psychology* (Middlesex, England: Penguin Books, 1953), 49.
9. See Morton Kelsey, *Dreams: A Way to Listen to God* (New York: Paulist Press, 1978).
10. Trina Paulus, *Hope for the Flowers* (New York: Paulist Press, 1972), 76.
11. Thomas Merton, *The Wisdom of the Desert* (New York: New Directions, 1960), 30.

12. Henry D. Thoreau, "Among the Worst of Men That Ever Lived," *Collected Poems of Henry Thoreau*, ed. Carl Bode (Baltimore: Johns Hopkins Press, 1964), 172.

13. Henry D. Thoreau, *The Writings of Henry D. Thoreau: Journal I*, ed. John C. Broderick (Princeton, N.J.: Princeton University Press, 1981), 385.

14. Quoted in Robert Bly, *The Winged Life: The Poetic Voice of Henry David Thoreau* (San Francisco: Sierra Club Books, 1986), 58.

15. Bly, *The Winged Life*, 52.

CHAPTER 2

1. Thomas Merton, *Contemplation in a World of Action* (New York: Image Books, 1973), 358.

2. John H. Westerhoff and John D. Eusden, *The Spiritual Life* (New York: Seabury Press, 1982), 75, 76.

3. See Martin Bell, *The Way of the Wolf: The Gospel in New Images* (New York: Seabury Press, 1968), 113.

4. Anne Wilson Schaef, *When Society Becomes an Addict* (San Francisco: Harper & Row, 1987), 24.

5. Schaef, *When Society Becomes an Addict*, 18.

6. Jones, *Journey into Christ*, 96.

7. Helen M. Luke, *Dark Wood to White Rose: A Study of Meanings in Dante's Divine Comedy* (Pecos, N.M.: Dove Publications, 1975), 42.

8. Eliot, "East Coker," 129.

9. Thomas Merton, *The Way of Chuang Tzu* (New York: New Directions, 1965), 24.

10. C. G. Jung, commentary on Richard Wilhelm's translation and explanation of *The Secret of the Golden Flower* (New York: Harcourt Brace Jovanovich, 1962), 93.

11. See *Breakthrough: Meister Eckhart's Creation Spirituality in New Translation*, introduction and commentary by Matthew Fox (Garden City, N.Y.: Image Books, 1980), 213–25.

12. M. Scott Peck, *The Road Less Traveled* (New York: Simon & Schuster, 1978), 19.

13. Luke, *Dark Wood to White Rose*, 39.

14. James Hillman, *Re-Visioning Psychology* (New York: Harper & Row, 1975), 69.

CHAPTER 3

1. *Breakthrough*, 103.

2. *Breakthrough*, 118.

3. See *Illuminations of Hildegard of Bingen*, commentary by Matthew Fox (Sante Fe, N.M.: Bear and Co., 1985), 64, 99, 113.

4. *Breakthrough*, 108.

5. Thomas Merton, *The New Man* (New York: Farrar, Straus & Giroux, 1961), 63.

6. Thomas Merton, *New Seeds of Contemplation* (New York: New Directions, 1961), 34.

7. *Fritz Kunkel: Selected Writings*, ed. with introduction and commentary by John A. Sanford (New York: Paulist Press, 1984), 25–26.

8. *Fritz Kunkel: Selected Writings*, 25.

9. *Fritz Kunkel: Selected Writings*, 23.

10. *The Collected Works of St. Teresa of Avila*, vol. 2, trans. Otilio Rodriguez and Kieran Kavanaugh (Washington, D.C.: ICS Publications, 1980), 286.

11. Linda Schierse Leonard, *On the Way to the Wedding: Transforming the Love Relationship* (Boston: Shambhala, 1987) 35–36.

12. Sören Kierkegaard, *Purity of Heart*, trans. Douglas V. Steere (New York: Harper & Row, 1938), 187.

13. Carol Pearson, *The Hero Within* (San Francisco: Harper & Row, 1986), 62.

14. Sam Keen, *The Passionate Life: Stages of Loving* (San Francisco: Harper & Row, 1983), 129–30.

15. Keen, *The Passionate Life*, 141.

16. Irene Claremont de Castillejo, *Knowing Woman: A Feminine Psychology* (New York: Harper & Row, 1973), 122.

17. Djohariah Toor, *The Road by the River: A Healing Journey for Women* (San Francisco: Harper & Row, 1987), 48–49.

18. Westerhoff and Eusden, *The Spiritual Life*, 22.

19. See Toor, *The Road by the River*, 49.

20. *Breakthrough*, 122.

21. See *Fritz Kunkel: Selected Writings*, 123–40.

22. Rollo May, *The Courage to Create* (New York: Bantam Books, 1975), 3.

23. Arthur Miller, *After the Fall* (New York: Viking Press, 1964), 24.

CHAPTER 4

1. Joseph Campbell, *The Hero with a Thousand Faces* (Princeton, N.J.: Princeton University Press, 1949), 91. See also p. 95, picturing the three panels of the "Night Sea Journey."

2. Daniel Levinson, *The Seasons of a Man's Life* (New York: Knopf, 1978), 20.

3. See Erik H. Erickson, *Childhood and Society* (New York: Norton, 1950), 247–74.

4. Levinson, *The Seasons of a Man's Life*, 30.

5. See Alan Jones, *Soul Making* (San Francisco: Harper & Row, 1985), 166–80.

6. John Sanford, *The Kingdom Within* (New York: Paulist Press, 1970), 66.

7. Martin Marty, *A Cry of Absence* (San Francisco: Harper & Row, 1983), 123.

8. Frank L. Baum, *The Wizard of Oz* (Chicago: Reilly and Lee, 1956), 14–15.

9. Eliot, "The Little Gidding," *The Complete Poems and Plays*, 145.

10. Pierre Teilhard de Chardin, *The Divine Milieu* (New York: Harper & Row, 1960), 89–90.

11. *Fritz Kunkel: Selected Writings*, 147.

12. e. e. cummings, "if I have made, my lady, intricate," *A Selection of Poems* (New York: Harcourt, Brace and World, 1965), 80.

13. Jones, *Soul Making*, 90–91.

14. C. G. Jung, *Memories, Dreams, and Reflections* (New York: Random House, 1961), 170.

15. *The Collected Works of St. John of the Cross*, book 2, trans. Kieran Kavanaugh and Otilio Rodriquez (Washington, D.C.: ICS Publications, 1979), 338.

16. Maria Edwards, "Midlife Crisis and the Dark Night," Contemplative Review, 16 (Summer 1983): 24.

17. C. G. Jung, *Man and His Symbols* (New York: Dell, 1964), 4.

18. Jean Houston, "Pathos and Soul Making," *Voices* 21 (Fall 1985–Winter 1986):73.

19. *Breakthrough*, 155–57.

CHAPTER 5

1. Thomas Kelly, *A Testament of Devotion* (New York: Harper & Brothers, 1941), 63; 58.

2. Daniel Day Williams, *The Spirit and the Forms of Love* (San Francisco: Harper & Row, 1968), 206.

3. Lewis Carroll, *Alice's Adventures in Wonderland* (New York: Random House, 1946), 50.

4. Kelly, *A Testament of Devotion*, 59.

5. Kelly, *A Testament of Devotion*, 61.

6. Merton, *New Seeds of Contemplation*, 251.

7. Merton, *New Seeds of Contemplation*, 256.

8. Merton, *New Seeds of Contemplation*, 258.

9. May, *The Courage to Create*, 4.

10. *Breakthrough*, 309.

11. Henri Nouwen, "A Spirituality of Waiting," *Weavings* 1 (Jan.-Feb. 1987): 14.

12. Nouwen, "A Spirituality of Waiting," 14.

13. Thomas Merton, *Thoughts in Solitude* (New York: Farrar, Straus & Giroux, 1956), 72.

14. O'Conner, *Our Many Selves*, 165.

15. *The Collected Works of St. Teresa of Avila*, 343–44.

16. Paulus, *Hope for the Flowers*, 75.

17. Alan Jones, *Passion for Pilgrimage* (San Francisco: Harper & Row, 1989), 83.

CHAPTER 6

1. Thomas Merton, quoted in Douglas Steere, *Together in Solitude* (New York: Crossroad, 1982), 118.

2. T. S. Eliot, "Burnt Norton," *The Complete Poems and Plays*, 119.

3. Gabriele Uhlein, *Meditations with Hildegard of Bingen* (Santa Fe, N.M.: Bear and Co., 1983), 90.

4. Quoted in Maggie Ross, *The Fire of Your Life: A Solitude Shared* (New York: Paulist Press, 1983), 64.

5. Rodney Clapp, "Eugene Peterson: A Monk Out of Habit," *Christianity Today*, Apr. 3, 1987, 25.

6. Janice Brewi and Anne Brennan, *Mid-life*, 115.

7. Jacob Needleman, *Lost Christianity: A Journey of Rediscovery* (San Francisco: Harper & Row, 1980), 165.

8. Henri Nouwen, *The Way of the Heart* (New York: Seabury Press, 1981), 72.

9. Brother Lawrence, *The Practice of the Presence of God* (Grand Rapids, Mich.: Baker Book House, 1975), 52.

10. Maggie Ross, *The Fire of Your Life*, 64.

11. Merton, *The Wisdom of the Desert*, 63.

12. Julian of Norwich, *Showings*, trans. Edmund Colledge and James Walsh (New York: Paulist Press, 1978) 159.

13. Samuel Beckett, *Waiting for Godot* (New York: Grove Press, 1954).

14. Marty, *A Cry of Absence*, 8.

15. Paul Tournier, *Secrets*, trans. Joe Embry (Richmond, Va.: John Knox Press, 1963), 59.

16. Henri Nouwen, *With Open Hands* (Notre Dame, Ind.: Ave Maria Press, 1972), 16, 154.

17. Jones, *Passion for Pilgrimage*, 45.

CHAPTER 7

1. Merton, *New Seeds of Contemplation*, 237.

2. Merton, *New Seeds of Contemplation*, 238.

3. Thomas Keating, *The Heart of the World* (New York: Crossroad, 1981), 69.

4. Toor, *The Road by the River*, 213.

5. Sue Woodruff, *Meditations with Mechtild of Magdeburg* (Sante Fe, N.M.: Bear and Co., 1982), 59, 60.

6. See *The Collected Works of St. John of the Cross*, 311.

7. Merton, *New Seeds of Contemplation*, 236.

8. Gerard Manley Hopkins, "The Wreck of the *Deutschland*," *The Poems of Gerard Manley Hopkins* (London: Oxford University Press, 1967), 63.

9. Rainer Maria Rilke, *Letters to a Young Poet*, trans. M. D. Herter Norton (New York: Norton, 1934), 35.

10. Quoted in *The Family Networker* 13 (January-February): 30.

11. Beatrice Bruteau, "Gospel Zen," *Living Prayer* 22 (July-Aug. 1989): 5.

12. Anthony de Mello, *The Heart of the Enlightened* (Garden City, N.Y.: Doubleday, 1989), 38.

13. *The Cloud of Unknowing*, trans. with introduction by Ira Progoff (Julian Press, 1957), 94.
14. Needleman, *Lost Christianity*, 172, 174.
15. *The Collected Works of St. John of the Cross*, 336.
16. Joseph Campbell with Bill Moyers, *The Power of Myth* (New York: Doubleday, 1988), 118.
17. Gibran, *The Prophet* (New York: Knopf, 1966), 29.
18. Shea, *Stories of God*, 31–32.
19. Rilke, *Letters to a Young Poet*, 65. The phrase "waster of sorrows" is from Rainer Maria Rilke, *Duino Elegies*, trans. J. B. Leishman and Stephen Spender (New York: Norton, 1963), 79.
20. Catherine of Siena, quoted in Madeleine L'Engle, *Irrational Season* (New York: Seabury Press, 1977), 28.
21. Marion Woodman, *The Pregnant Virgin* (Toronto: Inner City Books, 1985), 152.
22. Rilke, *Letters to a Young Poet*, 59.
23. Flannery O'Connor, "Parker's Back," *Everything That Rises Must Converge* (New York: Farrar, Straus & Giroux, 1956), 225.

CHAPTER 8

1. Paulus, *Hope for the Flowers*, 78.
2. Theophane the Monk, *Tales of a Magic Monastery* (New York: Crossroad, 1981), 33.
3. Murray Stein, *In Midlife* (Dallas: Spring Publications, 1983), 5–6.
4. *Spiritual Sayings of Kahlil Gibran*, trans. and ed. Anthony Rizcallah Ferris (New York: Bantam Books, 1962), 20.
5. The story appears in its original version in Henry D. Thoreau, *Walden*, ed. J. Lyndon Shanley (Princeton, N.J.: Princeton University Press, 1971), 333.
6. Westerhoff and Eusden, *The Spiritual Life*, 37.
7. Woodruff, *Meditations with Mechtild of Magdeburg*, 47.

8. Ann Belford Ulanov, *Picturing God* (Cambridge, Mass: Cowley Publications, 1986), 171.

9. Lorna Green, "The Femininity of God," *Contemplative Review* 16 (Summer 1983): 12.

10. *Illuminations of Hildegard of Bingen*, 23.

11. Alice Walker, *The Color Purple* (New York: Harcourt Brace Jovanovich, 1982), 167.

12. Gerard Manley Hopkins, "God's Grandeur," *The Poems of Gerard Manley Hopkins*, 66.

13. Keen, *The Passionate Life*, 200.

14. Keen, *The Passionate Life*, 52.

15. Jean-Pierre de Caussade, *Abandonment to Divine Providence*, trans. John Beevers (Garden City, N.Y.: Doubleday, 1975), 41, 52.

16. William Blake, "Auguries of Innocence," *Selected Poetry and Prose of Blake*, ed. Northrop Frye (New York: Modern Library, 1953), 90.

17. Martin Buber, *Tales of the Hasidim: The Later Masters* (New York: Schocken Books, 1948), 173.

18. Bruteau, "Gospel Zen," 8.

19. Eliot, "The Dry Salvages," *The Complete Poems and Plays*, 136.

20. Buber, *Tales of the Hasidim*, 251.

21. Paulus, *Hope for the Flowers*, 77.

22. Meister Eckhart, quoted in Lawrence LeShan, *How to Meditate* (New York: Bantam Books, 1974), 92.

23. Theophane the Monk, *Tales of a Magic Monastery*, 18.

24. Pierre Teilhard de Chardin, *The Divine Milieu*, 116.

25. Kelly, *A Testament of Devotion*, 99.

26. *Breakthrough*, 206.

27. Elie Wiesel, *Night* (New York: Avon Books, 1958), 109.

28. Annie Dillard, *Pilgrim at Tinker Creek* (New York: Harper & Row, 1974), 218.